To the born, the unborn, and the mothers. Whose joy suffers, who suffer joy.

NOTE
MID-
KAROLIN

S FOR
R O
IRTH
A ZAPA

Notes for Mid-Birth
by Karolina Zapal
© 2019

Notes for Mid-Birth is typeset in "antykwa Półtawskiego," a typeface designed by Polish typographer Adam Półtawski specifically for its performance with the Polish language. Given that Polish uses letters with significant diagonals (k, w, y, z) more frequently than English, the boldness of these features was downplayed to smooth out the overall imprint of text bodies on the eye. During the Nazi occupation of Poland, Półtawski organized and conducted secret underground graphic design workshops. Titles are set in "Interstate."

Designed by John Trefry for **Inside the Castle**.
Cover art drawn by Dunja Krcek, http://dunjakrcek.net/

Notes for Mid-Birth is the 21st book from
Inside the Castle and is part of the expanded field of literature.

ISBN 13: 978-1-7327971-6-1
www.insidethecastle.org / Lawrence, Kansas

In Karolina Zapal's stunning second book, a fevered momentum towards life beyond a womb of lukewarm freedom is suspended mid-birth as the landscape of borders rises to meet us— east/& west, woman/& womb, art/& artist. War breaks out at an intersection flung on the female form. People cross there. In this profound meditation on the borders of a body and the powers allowed to govern, Zapal contemplates the identity of a border, the ground it divides and the who that writes (rights) representation. Who gets to cross? Sometimes all you want to do in a poem is take a walk. Zapal is an insightful guide as she walks in tandem with her reader, examining with keen poetic brilliance the dilation of a country over generations, the churning of Poland's abortion laws, of protests, of histories and personal narratives. She leads us to the apex of a movement towards, never demanding we fall to one side or the other, but simply illuminating the profound space of in-between—how will we choose to deliver ourselves, our neighbors, the other, the other's body? Who even has choices?

- Marie Conlan author of *Say Mother Say Hand*
(Half Mystic, 2020)

Karolina Zapal's *Mid-Birth* asks us to not ask at all. Not to apologize, or expologize as Zapal calls it, but rather to seek virility through the tangible color of a movement. This is not to say a political movement necessarily, though it is always an option. Nor is it to say virility as masculinity, as in the broken men who have inherited war in their names, but virility as in the energy and creativity of a lightning strike, and how it makes offering, how it diagrams possibility; this text is a unique light in the inkiness of this heavy night.

By mapping histories of abortion debates in Poland/the U.S./ a female writer's body, the book also maps the (mis)use of the divine. Zapal translates between borders of women, countries, languages, and forms to create a kind of alchemy: the alchemy of envisioning the edges of the ungoverned womb. Let me ask you, dear reader, how do you paint liberation of a body, split? What names have you been forced to take? Hold this book up to help uncover another way.

- Shawnie Hamer, author of *The Stove is Off at Home*
(Spuyten Duyvil, 2018)

Fragile
is the earth above the springs: no tree should
be felled, no root
pulled up.

The springs might
dry up.

How many trees
are felled, how many roots
pulled up
within us?

(Reiner Kunze, tr. Mireil_e Gansel in *Translation as Transhumance*)

"Prawo" in Polish means both "law" and "right (direction)"

(insight by a prominent figure sewn into a burlap bag)

CONTENTS

NOTES FOR MID-BIRTH

1956 – Abortion is legalized for women with "difficult living conditions": for example, an entire family living in a single room or a woman sharing a flat with her in-laws without realistic hope of bettering her situation. It is up to a medical professional to decide whether she meets these conditions.

1959 – An executive order by The Ministry of Health further liberalizes abortion by allowing the woman seeking the abortion to evaluate her living conditions without seeking approval from a physician. Because of the "contraceptive Iron Curtain," behind which gynecologists deem domestically-manufactured contraceptives good for horses, but not humans, women turn to abortion as their primary means of birth control. Its legalization decreases the number of abortion-related deaths per year from 255 to twelve.

Laws remain more or less the same until after the fall of Communism. In 1990, new regulations limit access to abortion on social or economic grounds, making it obligatory to gain approval from four specialists, which restricts access especially to poor women in rural areas. They also introduce the "conscience clause," which allows a physician to refuse to perform an abortion if it is against one's morals.

1993 – The Act on Family Planning, Human Embryo Protection and Conditions of Permissibility of Abortion, otherwise known as the "anti-abortion" act, goes into effect. This act permits abortion only if the mother's life is in danger, the pregnancy results from incest or rape, or prenatal tests determine fetal abnormalities. Physicians can no longer perform abortions in private clinics. A fetus becomes known as an "unborn child" and gains citizenship rights that have the potential to overrule the mother's.

Under this law, the woman seeking the abortion is protected, not prosecuted. The responsibility falls on the person performing the abortion.

Although clamping down on abortion, the act calls for better access to birth control and the distribution of medical, legal, and social services to families pre- and post-partum. It forces schools to offer students maternity leave that won't delay their continued education and alternative test dates for important exams within a six-month window. The act also promotes human sexuality education, focusing on family values and the right to life of the unborn.

I was born, my birth coinciding with infamous act becoming law. My mother, a teacher, could have chosen to take up to three years of maternity leave.

1996 – Parliament votes to amend the recent law, once again allowing abortions to be performed on social and economic grounds. This action reinstates the right of private institutions to offer abortions and retires the fetus's status as an "unborn child."

1997 – But the amendment is not adequately implemented before the 1993 "anti-abortion" act resurfaces and becomes what will continue to govern Poland's abortion laws for over two decades.

2000 – Alicja Tysiąc, a woman suffering from severe myopia and a single mother of three, is refused an abortion after being warned by three specialists she may lose her eyesight if she carries to term. As expected, her eyesight drastically deteriorates after giving birth. She becomes legally disabled, requiring daily assistance.

2001 – The left comes back into power, running on a pro-choice campaign. However, the government quickly tables the abortion issue in exchange for the Polish Episcopate's support for Poland's accession into the European Union.

2003 – Under the influence of the Catholic Church, the Polish government asks EU councils for assurance that "no EU treaties or annexes to those treaties would hamper the Polish government in regulating moral issues or those concerning the protection of human life." In other words, Poland guarantees itself autonomy from the EU's regulations on abortion.

Tysiąc sues the Polish government for "the right to respect for private life," having been denied an abortion despite threats to her health.

2007 – The European Court of Human Rights rules in favor of Tysiąc and awards her €25,000 in damages. It also forces Poland to establish an appeals mechanism for when a disagreement arises between a woman and her doctor or between two doctors about whether a situation meets the legal qualifications for abortion. Among other things, it must consider the woman's view on the matter and must make a decision in a timely manner, such that, if the appeal results in the woman's favor, she may still have an abortion in the legally permitted window.

Shortly thereafter, the largest Catholic weekly magazine in Poland, the pleasantly named *Gość Niedzielny* (Sunday Visitor), publishes an editorial written by editor-in-chief Fr. Marek Gancarczyk, decrying the decision made by the court. In it, Gancarczyk compares the current abortion climate to the Holocaust: how Nazis used to drink after work, being desensitized to murder.

2009 – The Polish court fines the magazine over ten thousand dollars for publishing the offensive article. Outraged, the Catholic Church deems this an infringement of freedom of speech.

2014 – Pope John Paul II, born Karol Wojtyła, is canonized. In gratitude, three thousand of Poland's doctors nurses, and medical students sign a "declaration of faith," affirming they will not perform abortions, in-vitro fertilization, and euthanasia, nor recommend and prescribe birth control.

Later this same year, a woman is refused an abortion by the director of Warsaw's Holy Family hospital, Dr. Bogdan Chazan, who is one of the most notable supporters of the "conscience clause." The refusal comes towards the end of the legal termination window after the woman finds out her fetus suffers from serious malformations and will die soon after birth. She has no choice but to carry the baby to term. It dies nine days after delivery.

Warsaw mayor, Hanna Gronkiewicz-Waltz, fires Dr. Chazan for dismissing the woman's pleas for an abortion and for failing to refer her to another hospital or physician. This decision causes an uproar in the Catholic Church.

There are many stories like this one that don't make the news because women are scared to talk and do not pursue legal action. In May 2018, The Federation for Women and Family Planning initiates a #HistorieKobiet (women's stories) campaign to give women a platform to speak out about their experiences. Most stories come to them anonymously through the mail.

One woman's story made public by this campaign—translated and summarized—is this:

My husband and I try to conceive for a long time. When I finally become pregnant, the first doctor I see informs me the fetus I am carrying is malformed and refers me to the hospital for an abortion. There, doctors deceitfully assure me the baby's fine—they have the latest high-tech equipment, after all—and shame me for wanting to abort a healthy child. I celebrate without restraint. Around the sixth month of pregnancy, I begin to notice that not a single doctor will look me in the eye or react to stories about my preparations for the child. Eventually, one of them follows me into the hallway after a visit and yells, "You shouldn't be so happy because you are going to give birth to a very sick child who will not live very long." I am devastated, the pregnancy suddenly unbearable. I survive only because of my husband's unrelenting support. The child dies a few months after birth. My husband encourages me to take legal action, but I worry about once again "being thrown into shadows."

There are many stories like this one that the silence of fear overshadows.

2015 – The national-conservative Law and Justice party (PiS) comes into power, gaining the majority of seats in both the Sejm (lower house) and the Senate (upper house). This imbalance of political power makes it possible for them to push their own agenda unopposed. Many Poles become devoted supporters because of the party's commitment to tradition and national pride. They lower the retirement age and provide families with welfare benefits: 500zł per month per child (starting with their second onwards), which is about $130. However, their social policies are strictly conservative: pro-life and anti-LGBTQ+.

2016 – The Law and Justice party proposes a new "stop abortion" bill, even though Poland's abortion policies are already among the strictest in the EU. The bill would force women to give birth to malformed children, so they would receive a proper Catholic burial.

The punishments read as follows:

Three months to five years for having or performing an abortion (as opposed to 1993's "up to two years" for those performing an abortion and no legal consequence for those having an abortion).

Penalties also apply to anyone who encourages the abortion or helps in any way.

Up to three years for causing an abortion *bezmyślnie* (without thought).

Penalties do not apply if the abortion is caused accidentally by medical action trying to save the mother's life.

When it comes to the woman having an abortion, the court may soften or alleviate the sentence. However, she may still be imprisoned, which deviates from the 1993 law that does not punish her.

One to ten years for forcing a mother to abort her child.

One to ten years for performing an abortion that results in the mother's death.

Two to twelve years for forcing a mother to abort her child if she dies during the procedure.

Three years for harming the fetus.

One year for a mother who harms the fetus if she does it without thinking.

With these harsh sentencing laws, even physicians who aren't morally opposed to abortion refuse to perform the procedure. They do not want to put their careers or families at risk.

*

I'm sifting through legal terminology and translating it to English. "One must imagine Sisyphus happy," Camus says.

*

Taken from the 2016 bill:

Art. 1. Każdy człowiek ma przyrodzone prawo do życia od chwili poczęcia, to jest połączenia się żeńskiej i męskiej komórki rozrodczej. Życie i zdrowie dziecka od jego poczęcia pozostają pod ochroną prawa.

(Art. 1. Every person has an innate right to life from the moment of conception, meaning the joining of male and female gametes. The child's life and health, from the moment of conception, are under the protection of the law.)

The first translation I find for *przyrodzone* is "birthright," which correctly matches the literal translation of the word: *przy* meaning "next to" and *rodzone* meaning "birth." So, everyone has a right to life that's "next to" "birth," *not* any time before.

"Gametes," in the original Polish, are *komórki rozrodcze.*

I've always known *komórka*, or the plural *komórki*, to mean either "cell phone" or "pantry."

🔊 komórka (f)　　🔊 cell · chamber · cubby-hole · loculus · cell phone · cellphone · cellular · cellular phone · cellular telephone · mobile · mobile phone · mobile telephone

🔊 rozrodczy (adj. m)　　🔊 fertile · generative · procreative · reproductive · childbearing

Never with the word *rozrodcze*, which together can translate to "procreative" "cubby-hole."

But in the end, I understand: "reproductive" "cell." I also find that *komórka* is feminine. *Jaskinia* (cave) is feminine. *Dziura* (hole) is feminine. Anything that makes space for retraction is feminine; we retract our voices when we breathe. A phallic inhale.

*

October 3, 2016 – The "Black Protest" otherwise known as "Black Monday." Tens of thousands of men and women boycott work and school to protest the "stop abortion" bill. Streets in cities across Poland, including Warsaw, Kraków, and Wrocław, fill with black—clothing, umbrellas, signs, and smoke. Surprised by the unprecedented size of the crowd and echo-protests in Brussels, Berlin, and London, lawmakers backtrack. Parliament rejects the bill.

As a Polish immigrant in America, I find out about the protest last minute from a friend and chastise my ignorance. I see Polish American friends showing their support on social media, but I stir in silence; a post, from me, right now, would feel inauthentic.

At the time, I am working as a canvasser for the 2016 presidential election. Although affiliated with Hillary's campaign, my job is not necessarily to convince people to vote a certain way, but to convince them to vote: to show up at the polls, to mail in their ballots, to not abstain, thinking their votes won't matter. As I knock on strangers' doors by myself at night, I am preoccupied with American politics and my femaleness, the organization failing to offer any measures to make me feel comfortable and safe. I do things like interrupt band practice for a group of "dudes," who only laugh at my optimism and delight in theirs; attempt to speak to a woman whose bumper sticker, lawn post, and fridge magnet already suggest she won't be interested in speaking with me; furiously write an essay about the job titled "Ki$$ the President"—either "kill" or "kiss." I am met with a lot of aggression, both for questioning hard political ideologies and interrupting protected homelives. Only one person offers me water, says "thank you."

Guilt continues to sidle past my defenses. Why did I not learn about the "Black Protest" weeks in advance and hop on a plane? Why am I not there protesting with them, adorned in black garb? Then, upon reading news stories, guilt turns to sadness. Seeing women who look like me fight for the keys to their own bodies makes me cry. The whole thing feels like a ride through woods riddled with low-hanging branches that smother my vision; when it seems like they'll let up, another one smacks me in the face.

However, my non-attendance awakens my activism. The spinning bottle finally lands on something important for me to kiss.

2017 – The Federation for Women and Family Planning launches a campaign to combat a recently drafted bill by the Association of Polish Catholic Pharmacists that seeks to implement the "conscience clause" for pharmacists. If passed, it would allow pharmacists to refuse to stock and fill prescriptions for birth control if doing so pricks their conscience. It would affect specifically women in rural areas without alternatives to pharmacies operating under this clause. In August 2018, they have just over 11,000 signatures, short of their 15,000 goal. I sign it and post a link on Facebook, excited to help the organization gain their next few signatures. I only get one "like" from a Polish female friend, who, in the end, does not go on to sign the petition.

"Petitions on Facebook can be hard," a friend says in way of consolation. He signs the petition.[1]

July 23, 2017 – Restrictions are imposed on the "morning-after" pill, forcing women to obtain a prescription in order to purchase the drug.

September 2017 – Doctors across Poland form a group called *Lekarze Kobietom* (Doctors Help Women), which provides fast access to doctors willing to write prescriptions for the "morning-after" pill. While their website shows the towns where the doctors are located, they don't give out a doctor's information unless contacted by a woman in an emergency situation.

A woman has up to 120 hours after she has sex to take the pill, but the sooner she takes it, the better

[1] As of November 2019, the Association of Polish Catholic Pharmacists is still working on implementing the "conscience-clause" for pharmacists. The Federation for Women and Family Planning shuts down the campaign at 14,908 signatures.

it works. Within the network of these doctors who help women, the closest one to the rural village where I grew up is ninety km away. Since most pharmacies are closed on Sundays, this might require a woman needing the pill to skip work during a weekday, not to mention skirt any number of other responsibilities, like taking care of her children, to make the trip. If she doesn't have a car, which is true of forty percent of Poland's population (down from about eighty-five percent in 1990), the trek would be longer and more grueling. Google Maps cannot even establish a route using public transportation. She would have to ask family or friends for a ride or establish her own public transportation itinerary, which is sure to be involved and can get expensive.[2]

Early 2018 – A revised "stop abortion" bill, which eases the punishment on women for seeking an abortion but aims to eliminate prenatal screening to prevent women from being able to choose to abort on the grounds of fetal abnormality, penetrates Polish parliament.

March 22, 2018 – Over two hundred organizations from around the world sign a joint statement titled, *Polish Parliament Must Protect Women's Health and Rights*, urging the government to listen to the

[2] Since writing this in August 2018, the organization has added many more locations in which doctors are willing to write prescriptions for the pill. One of them is the larger town where people in my village go to shop for groceries. It is only fifteen km away.

voices of women in Poland and reject the proposal. "We are deeply concerned," it begins.

March 23, 2018 – "Black Friday," and not the kind Americans know. Again, thousands of men and women wearing black take to the streets of Poland to protest the latest bill.

It sits in limbo. I check headlines daily, bracing myself. For a long time, there's nothing new. Then predictions begin to circulate: if the Law and Justice party wins the parliamentary election in October 2019, as projected, the bill will be passed.

October 12, 2019 – On this sunny autumn afternoon, a friend and I drive two hours to Lawrenceville, Georgia to cast our votes in the parliamentary election. The polls are held in the basement of a church named after a Canadian nun. In the parking lot, a flock of black suits are carrying a dental-white coffin. To where? Supposedly where it's scheduled to be, and paid for. There is no wind. The Polish flag hangs stale in the doorway, and I think its fat red stripe and white stripe can easily be removed from what the two symbolize together to then mean: nothing. A color can easily lose its meaning when it's dependent on another. So can a person.

The ballot is so long it hangs off the voting podium, tickling my thighs, like a little girl's dress if she were sitting there, recording my vote. A rough piece of white cardboard surrounds my body to give me privacy, like a dressing room curtain. Am I undressing? In a way, by making choices, I am. But I am not ashamed of my vote, rather of my broken Polish. My eyes cross as I read the dozens of candidates' names across five parties and instructions on how to vote, riddled with accent marks. That is how I find myself naked; that is what needs cover. My compatriot carpool cat finishes quickly. I think for another minute, make my marks, and leave.

The election is supposed to be a blowout: the Law and Justice party will maintain their majority in both the upper and lower houses and with it, their iron grip on the country. However, the opposition fights like hell: not for any one party to win majority over PiS—that is next to impossible—but to prevent PiS from winning majority. The three main leftist parties, The Democratic Left Alliance, Spring, and Left Together, even unite, forming *Lewica* or "The Left" in order to clear the threshold (five percent of the vote) to get any seats at all. It works—partially. While PiS retains majority in the Sejm, they win the same number of seats as in 2015 with higher voter turnout. Additionally, they lose the majority in the Senate albeit by the narrowest margin: out of one hundred seats, PiS takes forty-nine, and the opposition, fifty-one.

From a pessimist's standpoint, this isn't ideal. PiS still controls the more powerful house of the Polish government, solidifying their rule. But from an optimist's, it's a victory or at least a step in the right direction. The loss of majority in the Senate will make it harder for PiS to make new laws, like those that limit women's reproductive rights.

Again I wait. Waiting is hard. It is one of the hardest activities, even if it's just waiting for a bus or for him to finish brushing his teeth and get in bed. But, in this case, waiting for news means freedom from what the news can bring.

The women perform masculine protest. Perform "ness," approach "ness" to something greater, more equal. Every verb finds "ness" to become a noun, then enters a thesaurus when you're tired. Women are tired. They're all named Ness.

◆ *under protest*	niechętnie
◆ *under protest*	protestując

1. niechętnie *(zostawać):*	
◆ niechętnie	reluctantly
◆ niechętnie	unwillingly

2. niechętnie *(usposobiony):*	
◆ niechętnie	with an unfriendly attitude

You are late to your *activism*. The active activism away from writing. "Reluctantly" and "unwilling-ly"—curious translations; passion drives protest but protest itself is unwillingness. A teenager filling out an "about me" worksheet, under "hobbies," writes "protesting." You wonder if she's fueled by social conscience or teenage stubbornness.

Living with yourself gets a whole lot harder when you're constantly needing to decide: whose side are *you* on? What time do you shut off the noise, concentrate without light? But, like most people at most parties, no one sees you in the corner poisoning your body.

Time gives you back seven hours when you're a little girl, which means you sleep through the protest. The protesters suffer alone. Native ghosts like you write about them, but this doesn't make them famous. For three years, you write about them. In that time, you can become a Catholic nun or train for a marathon, but instead, you feign wind. Which is nothing like running a marathon. And then you swing by too late, like a paling forecast. People already stand naked in their bathtubs, making time their God. Time visits everyone equally, for twenty-four hours a day. It's what people do with their time and at what age they die that makes time (God) inequitable. That and where their bodies body.

A body bodies waiting for a court ruling to unspool. Time becomes wait-time, thins out and lengthens, crushing the body in time.

Bottoms up to a privilege clock. It changes automatically when you land. Where you land changes.

Snow whitens the landscape, but it doesn't clear. Guilt. You feel for not learning about the fight until it's over(t), which isn't guilt at first, rather a sense that something's missing, like the back of an earring. Your fingers drift to it instinctively. The ocean grits its teeth, then spits out rinds of time.

Nostalgia thick as fog becomes tangible in your country. Your country? Your closet.

You try to write on the thin skin peeled off a mushroom. Your lover, this funguy illusion. You don't know how to freely give / birth or believe in misc / marriage, only how to be alone with a screen, thinking about islands. Poland is an island. It's so closet to German, yet so far away.

You've been Polish for only a few hours now. Before, you were Catholic. But for the sake of fairness, you gave him Jewish, and he gave you Polish. Your imagined future kids couldn't be two-thirds you (Polish *and* Catholic) and one-third Jewish since Jewish doesn't belong to a single nationality, not since the war, not in America. Was this Compromise? Removing religion like a stamp from a passport, from where you've been? All the pews you sat in, humming the songs and listening to your mother tell you, "If you're not going to sing, don't open your mouth at all"? To make yourself feel better, you estimate other couples' fractions: religion plus nationality, between the two of them. Are they four? You were three, and three was bad. Now you're two: half his ego and half your blood.

A detour into what checks out

✓ If both parties raising a child identify only with their (separate) nationalities, the children are half one party and half the other party.

✓ If both parties identify with their (separate) religions, but not with their nationalities because they're a bag of loose ends, the children are half one party and half the other party.

✓ If both parties identify with their (separate) nationalities and with their (separate) religions, the children are still half one party and half the other party.

✕ It gets complicated when parties share a nationality or a religion or both, like your parents: both Catholic Poles. Then you are whole mother's, whole father's, until you give up your Catholicism. Then you are half mother's and half father's.

✕ It also gets complicated when one party and the other do not operate under the same number of identifiers. If one party identifies strongly with a nationality and/or religion, and the second party does not identify with either, the children are wholly one party.

✕ If one party identifies strongly with a nationality, but not a religion, and the second party identifies with both a nationality and religion, the children are

two-thirds the other party. These are the hypothet-
ical calculator children who are misfit enough to
break a relationship heading for marriage.

All this assuming things get passed "on" to kids. A lot
more effort in the preposition. See: pass "by."

How late into the night do trucks barrel along. This
is a rhetorical question; the question mark is useless.
You have overexplained the previous page to death?
An indecisive statement is a rhetorical question.

You realize too late you forgot your coffee in Catholicism. You ruin sleepovers attempting to conjure up sympathy: if you could bring only one item to Catholicism, what would it be? A large boat? HA-HA. A quote etched in concrete outside your apartment says, "Noah didn't start building the ark in the rain," an aphorism. A Magic 8-Ball? John said this. "My sources say no." And then what if you forgot it when you left? Most likely someone forgot the government in Catholicism, or there'd be more separation between state and

church (which, in Poland, has the authority to deem August alcohol abstinence month and keep teaching religion in public school).

"I go to church for God, not for religion," your grandmother says.

You didn't know God was a state.

You text your roommate about the coffee, and she replies with a GIF of Jesus pouring it over his head in what appears to be a sensual bath. His glasses spill. He never finds them again and spends the rest of his days prophesying at -4.5, a trees-in-the-distance kind of blind.

Solutions:

1. Correct his vision

    Maybe some selfless kid will fetch him corrective lenses as his one and only item. Maybe the protests are that selfless kid, helping a friend out. And maybe the prescription just isn't strong enough yet.

2. Increase the image

    The more people who gather
        the larger the cloud of smoke.

3. Lure him closer

    "We're not asking you to save us, but to save us, you must first come down."

During the Compromise, you're ignorant to what you're wearing, like a child dressed in advertising. What you're wearing is his bushy jealousy, which agitates your soft skin, leaving floral rashes. A physical change you can't feel transpires near the roots, like getting a haircut. Your Sundays die off and resurrect as birds. Make a pie! They'll come to rest in a hot, sweet place. An autumn porch breathes longingly for all of your identities. You analyze the mailman, a jogger, a dog; they've surely endured compromises themselves and a part of them has been stripped. But which part? To find out, you use the three words for "miracle" in the Bible: "power," "sign," and "wonder." You dig in the mailman's body; he digs in yours. Maybe it's consent. You make a "follow me" sign, but the jogger simply keeps on jogging. You wonder about the dog, and this seems to work. The dog is now a hundred different manifestations of herself, each one less attractive than the last. In one of the manifestations she is Catholic again, and you are happy knowing at least you live wholly there. Your throat begins to itch like a shaved pubic area, mother to a new feral noise.

You feel whole when you travel, but you're only allowed a certain kind of wholeness. You're singing a song, with the refrain:

I'm jumping beds as if I were jumping lovers, but I'm jumping towns, no need for scissors...

In May 2018, Ireland votes to repeal the Eighth Amendment, legalizing abortion. In August 2018, Argentina rejects a bill to allow abortion in the first fourteen weeks of pregnancy. Women everywhere are fighting to become or remain whole. Even though the laws in America are also turbulent, you are, for the most part, looking at bruises in a gallery, rather than feeling them radiate with pain when they're poked. You have your parents to thank for that. And yet, Poland rents an expensive place in your heart. As in, it costs a lot for upkeep. When Poland insists on making decisions for the town, in this case, your body, neighbors, in this case, your organs, attempt extermination by flood and fire, leaving cracks in the wall and dress-forms of ash. Soon, you're pleading with Poland to vote in the town's favor, not in the favor of a few wooden boards and nails that might one day become a house. Other towns, in this case, your friends, choose to evict Poland, or otherwise, evacuate. Move the whole elsewhere, limb by limb,

breaking down in the process.

In middle school, the boy you like asks, "Want to know the secret to how I get my hair so smooth?" "I don't repeat." But history repeats. History hangs in knots on cafe walls, and you never know when someone will come along and order it instead of coffee because no one wants someone's weak Catholic leftovers.

Maybe, "as they say, history does not repeat itself, but it rhymes" (Margaret Atwood, *The Testaments*). Maybe the boy you like in middle school does not repeat, but dries, rhymes, nurses his hair like a babysitter, not a mother. So the results are the same.

All Polish colors are entities. Adjectives but also nouns. Their job (like a human has a job) is to describe objects—*czarne* chair, *czarny* tail—but they, themselves, are entities: *czerń*. English is deficient in colors with a soul; they become red "ness," pinkness, or yellowness, which no one ever says. Why did English-makers stop at "ness"? They weren't able to imagine anything better to name the noun, not even an amputated version of the adjective, like "pin" for pink or "yell" for yellow? (In Polish, *różowy*, pink, an adjective and a noun, also becomes *róż*, pinkness, a noun). That's why, in Poland, The Black Protest is less a protest where people wear black and more an entity—blackness—that wafts into the tenant.

If ten women wear a black dress, they're equally important. If ten women wear a red dress, they blend in. You learn this on The Bachelor. To try to understand, you listen to the heart of a television and that of a vagina, red and porch-like. When the screen is black, the news is the same. Viewers consider it of equal importance. If vaginas, however, looked and felt the same . . .

What if women had the ability to choose their vaginas based on what felt good and impressed sexual partners?

They don't like wearing the same dress, so imagine the horror if they chose the same vagina.

"Sexuality is not the most intractable element in power relations, but rather one of those endowed with the greatest instrumentality: useful for the greatest number of maneuvers and capable of serving as a point of support, as a linchpin, for the most varied strategies."

(Michel Foucault, *The History of Sexuality*)

Except how they use those same vaginas—those instruments—would still differ wildly.

Let's try a different analogy.

Gloomy weather, something flying over something else. Shadows sneaking in before true nightfall. Your grandfather paces to the end of the driveway and back again, on the lookout for thievery by the sky. He's more afraid of storms that come from the west—hills there. And then, suddenly, a red streak of light or something else red, unexpected, like blood in stool, shrieks in front of his vision. Shock, a call to the police, a doctor, maybe. There isn't supposed to be red in a storm, or, for that matter, a mushroom.

Black already blends in. Red is meant to stand out.   Too much red blends in. A lot of black stands out.

Colors are not transitive verbs—used with object. Perhaps, then, "black" doesn't need "ness" to have a soul, and the prerequisite for soul is to not come before an object.

Blue is like black in that there's strength in quantity. You write in an entirely blue room in a medical school, and you're not kidding about the floor and the chairs and the cubicles and the walls and the light waffles. You cannot open your kettle because it's too not blue. *You* because you're not conforming blue. Roller coaster blue, the color a container for stress.

Not many things are naturally blue except, of course, the sky, the water, the hottest part of fire. As a result, English-makers, when they got to the blueberry, decided to highlight "blue," even though the blueberry is only truly blue when you squint at a freshly picked basket in energetic sunlight. In Polish, blueberry is *jagoda* or *borówka*—a regional difference—neither of which index the color blue. By this logic, the Black Protests emphasize the scarcity of the color black in politics. Not enough anarchism.

Conceivably the protestors wear black for silence because silence creates new surfaces for reconditioning. (And you are the one brainstorming hypotheses about the map of creation, as if the black were an abstract memorial constructed by a sly architect.)

Or they wear black for bold. Like a mole springing up somewhere unwanted in one of the body's many meadows. The mole is bold. Goes where many tattoos do not dare go. It directs many gazes to it, gazes that revere its bravery but work to move it slightly off-center to better fit the eye.

As with vaginas, there's a dressing room for this, too. People try the protestors on, and they try them off.

Does squinting at a single blade of grass on a table illuminate more about grass than watching it grow outside?

Your grandmother asks you to cut the grass before you leave the country, but you forget. This illuminates more about guilt, which you'll get to later.

Black, the idea of it, has to first form in someone's mind. One person's. Unless two people think of it simultaneously. Chimneys, ones that stare at each other, must think alike in black.

"Hey, what about black?"
"No, too city. We don't want to scare the villagers."

Even people who come up with colors for a protest must face rejection, you think. Less than chimneys, though. No one likes a chimney. But there's no need to be scared. Everyone knows just as little as you do. How air travels without a passport.

And some animals aren't all that intuitive. Take for example a cat that will not pass through a hole when the flap is down, even if you drive its head through it to show it the way. No entrance, blacked out, end of story.

In the spring, the streets rupture, causing blood to sputter maroon and pink. The colors are mother and daughter, like the skin and seeds of a pomegranate. Their tint depends not on the species of blood, but on the sun's reach. In turn, the sun's reach depends on the configuration of buildings—which either suspend light at the height at which one can still make out a rogue balloon or let it fall to the grass and illuminate the earth. This depends on architects and city planners, whose jobs depend on there being something to plan. This is where civilization began: a plan, a plan to stop motion, which ironically moved motion forward. Bodies wearing black may have not been touched by the sun, but this, too, depends on how the city has treated them—obscuring them? —and the men that came before them, armed with a plan.

You ask her to get a massage with you because you feel silly doing it alone. She says, "Wow that's cheap," but doesn't follow through. She is touched by the sun, then forgets. Everyone is striped. When people gather, cars cross. The new Catholic cross is actually a person wearing a hat, blinking out the sun. This time the backdrop to the crucified body can feel pain. It gets nailed.

"Love comes from the mouth or in the heart / open on both ends, a tunnel" (Max Ritvo, *The Final Voicemails*). The throat is not a beachgoer. Love enters the mouth of the sea and travels to the heart, or it strikes the heart and rides the waves to be released out the mouth.

She wears white stripes, so the rest of her can remain black.

Google helps to piece together symbols. Death makes mourning makes rebirth makes sophistication possible. And a dark-silt fertility; you like how it sounds, cavernous and deep. Can death be fertile? A friend picks up a pamphlet at a religiously affiliated bookstore; it says, "Did Jesus really die?" And someone writes a good rhyming poem about a boring mass.

Does sexuality lead to fertility? Evolutionarily, the more sexual a woman is, the more chances she has to get pregnant, so shouldn't we admire high doses of sexuality? You learn a lot on The Bachelor.

But having a chance at showing "off" one's fertility doesn't match actually being fertile. Just like having a chance at showing off one's dance moves doesn't necessarily prove one's talent for dance.

Next.

Black packaging is for sleek packaging. Black clouds are for bad clouds.

Asphalt absorbs radiation and emits it as heat due to a low albedo. While it may sound like libido, the Latin root is *albus*, as albumen, the white of an egg. So you agree with the first part, when women are made to absorb too much toxicity, they emit fire. But it's not because of a low albedo.

You stumble upon a blog titled *the barren years*. Its author talks about getting to the point in her infertility where she has started to speculate whether the color of her underwear affects her chances to conceive. The comments on the post chronicle many experiments with colored undergarments. Someone asks if *plaid* works. Black doesn't make the cut.

If it were up to you, the most fertile color would be blackberry. Such a supple color, grasping sunshine in fists. Grows into late summer, when the world releases an egg and welcomes you to vacation in its heightened basal body temperature. When lightning strikes, because what first comes to mind is something phallic, the blackberries sing a tune. Even the young ones that look like brains wish the rain luck.

A few months later, a natural spring of blood drips,

                                                    drips.

You wish your period came in *snow*.

Pre-mourning: a sting swimming between your ribs; you can bat it with a single thought, a thought that acts, that "laments the passing of time." You have been pre-mourning your grandparents ever since your grandmother nonchalantly asked whether you wanted to see their reserved graves, as if what they reserved were seats for a flight across the Atlantic. Did they choose the window plot-with-a-view? Or the aisle for accessibility? Definitely not the middle; middle won only during sleepovers when you were little, as it guaranteed safety from supposed intruders.

At the time, you reviled the morbid question but recently went looking for the plots yourself. Maybe seeing them in person would plant them in the past, even temporarily, or rather lurch them far into the future. You did this on the off chance the surreal couldn't be real. In the end, they stayed put.

You go to Europe for a year to be closer to them. Your unemotional cousin, who lives in Germany, a more conveniently traversed distance away, but is on a stint in California working as an au-pair, texts you when you're with them. "How are they?" she asks. "But how's their health?"

Your mother staggers for the phone whenever she dreams about them, assuming her dreams are winning lottery numbers clicking into place.

You leave, not knowing what the reasons will be

behind your next arrival. The protesters pre-mourn. You have not yet taken to wearing black because, unlike the protesters, you pre-mourn specific people; a uniform color would target them.

This reason, yes, fits like a glove,

all the while missing the hand.

Women tend to apologize. I toss apologies here and there, as if playing ring toss to win the world. I do not aim at a singular target. I pick up ducks with colored dots that mean something—different reasons to feel guilty. And guilt trips, though they are trips, burrow me in inner-city ground floor hotel rooms, where the view is dark and damp; frankly there is no view at all. Women, my apologies. I am #sorry-notsorry for the #sorrynotsorry movement, which did not win the war on apology, only equipped the troops with a bossier attitude. People who interact with me, including women, take my apologies for granted; another shipment lies in wait.

The apology epidemic extends to women writers, specifically those writing nonfiction. They provide disclaimers for their work in case something goes wrong, someone finds issue. The disclaimers almost never take on common apologetic terminology, like "sorry" or "forgive me," though some do. Many readers drift past them because they read more like explanations. Many *are* explanations. I find them everywhere. I call them "expologies." On one hand,

I admire authors' being able to recognize potential holes in their work: a missing perspective, inaccessible or inaccurate information, imperfect terminology. On the other, I am concerned they prematurely apologize for what, in most cases, is hard, vulnerable criticism of the subject at hand. Criticism that's probably already less holey than others since the sport of apology is awareness.

It has been possible for me to accrue a sizable list of expologies in the course of a month just by reading—not researching, not *trying* to find them. And because there's a cap to how much I can read, the expologies are widespread. I shouldn't have been able to come across this many in this short amount of time.

Chimamanda Ngozi Adichie, in her book, *Dear Ijeawele*, writes a letter to a friend answering her question about how to raise her daughter feminist. Not far into the book, Adichie proclaims, "I have some suggestions for how to raise Chizalum. But remember that you might do all the things I suggest, and she will still turn out to be different from what you hoped, because sometimes life just does its thing" (9). An expology bares its two front teeth.

To ensure against blame for an adult female who shuns feminism, Adichie demeans the sensible female-empowered book to "some suggestions" that, in the end, might not even work. What this does is acknowledge that one cannot always protect against the world's whims, especially in how they affect those around us. However, because everyone regularly concedes to the world's whims, anyway, Adichie's explicit concession is redundant. What are the chances that in twenty years "Ijeawele" will blame Adichie for providing null suggestions? She has followed them precisely, only to find what, an autonomous woman on the other end? The chances are slim. No one should have to confirm the world's unpredictability in order to make suggestions. It's a given that not all ideas will breed perfect results.

But this exzology, at least, is not as bad as I initially expect. Because as soon as I read the first sentence, "I have some suggestions for how to raise Chizalum," I guess the rest: "but she's your child, and you can raise her however you see fit," which would underestimate the role of female support networks in raising a child.

Svetlana Alexievich, in *The Unwomanly Face of War: an Oral History of Women in World War II*, says, "I understand that I am dealing with versions, that each person has her version" (xxi), to communicate she is behind the women's "lies." She knows her interviewees are not providing textbook descriptions of war, and by acknowledging this, she shows people, shows men, she isn't playing their ballgame. They shouldn't get their pants in a bunch about her not scoring any goals with history. She isn't wont to iron. Her game doesn't involve shooting systemically validated facts into female-resembling receptacles.

Her game recruits players based on their life stories, and the back-and-forth is simply a conversation. She explains this, so people won't come explaining back. Even though the book as a whole is unapologetic in its style—which leans away from comprehensive-historical and focuses more on "small great human beings" (xxviii)—the above quote serves the purpose of getting people off her back. If people who are versed in winner's history challenge the book's contents, she can point them back to it: "I understand that I am dealing with versions," which suggests, "not the version everyone knows as the truth." But by saying this in the introduction, before giving readers a chance to read the oral histories themselves, she fictionalizes the women's truth. She counts on other versions.

The anthology that explores the many faces of the abortion movement in Ireland, *Repeal the 8th*, edited by Una Mullally, disclaims the following in its introduction: the book "is not a history of the movement for reproductive rights in Ireland, nor an academic study. It is not polemic nor a debate" (1).

And: "This collection of work is free-flowing, and purposefully uses a thematic narrative over a linear one [...] as a result, this anthology is purposefully inconclusive" (2).

I am grateful to have every single one of these books in my hands. The women who write them are fierce, knowledgeable, and unstoppable. Chimamanda Ngozi Adichie is an award-winning author and speaker. In one of her bone-chilling TED talks, she leads the audience through the many changes to her "feminist" identity in Nigeria—first "a happy feminist" to combat the misconception that feminists are unhappy and then "a happy Nigerian feminist" to challenge the West's monopoly on feminism. Svetlana Alexievich won the 2015 Nobel Prize in Literature. She invented her own nonfiction genre, processing oral histories to "build temples out of our feelings' (xxi). Una Mullally, in partnership with the crowd-funding publisher Unbound, worked to publish an outstanding collection of voices from the Repeal frontlines, a true feat in the face of opposition. Yet she uses the word "purposefully" in her introduction in case someone calls out what may appear to be stylistic "accidents," instead of letting the book speak for itself. Books take time and hard work. They're inherently purposeful.

A step further in the book, in an essay titled *Abortion, Regret and Choice*, Kitty Holland states, "I had not, however—and forgive me if I was not listening well enough—heard enunciated the reasons women choose abortion" (45). Holland aims to improve the Repeal movement by opening people's eyes to what might be missing from its charge but undercuts her own opinion to soothe those who may think she's wrong. She makes a point and then immediately retracts it. She does this presumably because she knows she hasn't read every book, skimmed every pamphlet, shown up at every protest, and scoured every website, every blog, every forum that might have mobilized the missing focus—the reasons women choose abortion. She does what she can, and she knows it may not be enough to form a foolproof critique. It is possible sources detailing "why" exist. But does this warrant an expology? Anyone involved in a large national campaign for change is bound to miss something.

*

And here I am, aching to write an expology, one that tells readers everything this book is not, under my keen supervision. I defend, "Yes, men also expologize, but I have noticed this more in women." When I find a Rebecca Solnit quote in *Men Explain Things to Me* that backs me up—"The out-and-out confrontational confidence of the totally ignorant is, in my experience, gendered" (4), or, in other words, non-confrontational non-confidence is gendered—I feel relieved.

I know nothing about writing a feminist text. Or, I don't know everything, which translates to my knowing nothing. I have friends with bigger feminist personas that could easily take my place in writing this and do it well. What I have going for me is the heart-stock I have invested in Poland—enough for a substantial stew—and a student's ability to research. I have never been or ever tried to get pregnant (and I'm not saying this to appease pro-lifers, but to corroborate my lack of knowledge with my lack of experiences. I did not attend the Black Protests. My non-attendance is what spawned the guilt that began this book that now calls for an expology.

I agonize over the infertility blog for a long time, wondering whether *my* stance on abortion negatively affects those trying to conceive. Not my stance, specifically but groupthink. This ultimately undermines my credibility in writing a largely pro-choice poetic experiment (though it's *not* a debate over sides). I take a walk through the woods' arteries with a friend. He says, "I never imagined you'd be saying this about the one opinion you said you'd never change." The one opinion that's becoming a book.

But I return to my sources and once again confront the consequences of abortion's illegality. Not only does a lack of accessible abortion affect trust, but also sexuality, and consent, and health, and class, and money, and politics, and religion. There are women who cannot get pregnant and women who do not want to be pregnant. Any link between them is artificial, made up for a cause, for the media, calling on the conscience.

I'm scared to tell my mother (my own loving, yet? very Polish mother) that I'm writing a book about Poland's abortion laws. I've never spoken to her about abortion, so I estimate her reaction based on Poland's laws, our Catholic religion. I settle for saying I'm writing a book about women's rights. "How do you know anything about women's rights?" she asks. The "you" she uses is the same "you" I use, the same distance behind. Even if I do communicate the full truth, and she buys it (on sale), I would have to explain to her why I'm not saying it straight. Why I'm not writing a book that will sell. Because it's *not* about that, Mom.

*

Other apologies:

1.   I've made a beeline for marriage, like a captain with weak peripheral vision. Recently I've gone off to explore the islands, my stagnant compliance with my past "boy craziness" dragging after me in the sand. What I mean is, I once found it odd that Game of Thrones didn't follow the trajectory of a single important romance; when my friends stated the show just wasn't *about love*, I found it ludicrous, something not being *about love*. This might qualify as feminism-lite.

2.   I look to happily unmarried women in their thirties like Pinocchio looks to real boys. They are goddesses who have figured out the secret formula to life, yet I cannot focus long enough to reach the same conclusion. Sometimes there's lying involved, and a whole lot of growing.

3.   I come up with sea and land analogies to nail down pre- and post- marital spaces. I'm so embarrassed by this I (mostly) cut them out of point #1.

4.	I'm in that stage of my ex-relationship where we still provide each other with services.

5.	Friends have confided in me about their miscarriages and abortions, and I have blindly reduced them to those experiences. Orbs in the audience. At a poetry reading, a woman reads a viscerally detailed poem about a miscarriage, and I look around frenziedly for sadness adorning a fragile face.
6.	I am largely ignorant of the desperation that may accompany the desire to conceive when unable.

7.	I don't know whether I should be apologizing for questioning my beliefs.

8.	A sitting contract for this book calls for my spending unapologetic time polishing it up. But I feel far from the activism, from the moment of fervor that led me to write it in the first place.

9.	I write better in comfortable chairs. Facing windows. I come up with all sorts of excuses.

10.	Something eventually comes, but not until after I pace two studio rooms sealed with white planks and cobwebs, reading Adichie and sipping a concoction of peppermint tea and instant coffee that I set up for myself on an easel. Blood and coffee stain the radiator. The weather is not surprising (and I like when weather surprises me). How obvious it is that I'm not doing the *real* work.

And then there are the fictitious solutions I imagine that don't help anyone. They're not sarcastic or ironic, just runs of the imagination that maybe aren't even art. Examples:

What if it were men who passively "got pregnant" instead of actively impregnating? Would the abortion debate still exist? Helen Linehan, in *Repeal the 8th*, says, "I swear, if men could have babies, there'd be an abortion app" (20). I want to put this through science, though it would be hard to test. The experiment would call for genetically engineering men to have all the right parts and then sending them, along with a group of women who already have the right parts, beyond the laboratory, into conditions under which they'd consider abortion an option. Once there, they'd be met (and judged) by two groups: a group whose thoughts have been wiped and who have been quarantined, away from society's expectations; and a group already imbued by today's "rules." In the end, would we be calling everyone a hypocrite?

What if the church paid unmarried couples for every day they weren't pregnant? Would this help the campaign for abstinence? Probably not. For protection, maybe. Men would complain less about having to wear condoms if wearing them increased their allowance. Another idea: what if parents made condoms readily available? A cookie jar turned condom jar. These ideas seem as decent as paying one's child five cents per page to read—Adichie's feminist suggestion.

"What are you reading?" a friend asks me. Referring to *Repeal the 8th*, I say, "The Eighth Amendment." I think, what if everyone read The Constitution, mastered the law? On a bus tour to the Cliffs of Moher, I learn about a woman who found a legal loophole that allowed her ten months with each man she married without having to give up her property, which she wanted to pass down to her son; she married and divorced many times. With abortion, people would study the law not necessarily to find loopholes, but to substantiate arguments. Either way, they'd need to outsmart the government.

*

It's easier to be unapologetic in fiction. An author does not introduce a plot by explaining it or apologizing for the twists and turns. She does not say, "Forgive me, for I have created a character who rarely offers one's sympathy, can be rude at times, and assumes cats are reincarnated kings." The character can pass a row of dying sunflowers without lifting a finger, indulge in apathy, or otherwise resolve to help the starving dogs she sees on TV. No one expects the character to abide to a truth that women nonfiction writers apparently cannot grasp.

Repeal the 8th features a short story by Tara Flynn titled *Three: three*. In it, Flynn approaches abortion from three different perspectives: that of a young woman traveling from Ireland to the U.K. for an abortion, that of a religious woman in her fifties, a mother of daughters, who resents how pro-choice campaigns treat the church, and that of a cocky, disrespectful young man undeserving of his privilege to "sit out" during an abortion. This last narrative is shocking, sickening. I read it and react out loud, which usually only happens when my reaction is good. Here is an excerpt:

The truth? I don't care. Not personally, not really. I don't care what sluts do, with who or where they do it, or whether they get pregnant or stay pregnant or not. Condoms? Me? Nah. Never liked the feel. And if some bitch lets things get that far, doesn't look out for herself, then why would I look out for her? I'm not her husband. Husband? Who'd marry a slut like her? She'll die alone, the libtard bitch. Haha.

Told you I didn't care. I don't care.

I don't like posting harsher stuff when Mam's downstairs. She'd never see it – she won't go online, I do all her emails – but I still don't like the feeling. She taught me right, my Mam. I know how to treat a lady. A decent one. One who deserves it. What the fuck happened to decency, ha? To traditional values? I'm not the one who's out of step. It's the world that's gone mad.

Girls I know, ones I went to school with, like, we made our communion and our confirmation to-

gether (oh, they don't like religion but they took the cash quick enough, didn't they?), they're not one bit afraid to say the most disgusting things now. To wear words on their chests that might as well say 'Murder' and it's getting out of hand. We will need strong hands to get things back to how they were. I'll be those hands. What's right is right. (188)

The text is surely brutal enough to warrant an expology. It is written by a woman digging into a man's head, which could be considered a crime. And yet, the author lets it speak for itself; readers let the author let it speak for itself. As a reader, I am glad there isn't an expology (or a trigger warning, which has the potential to become an expology). So the question is: why is it exempt? Because even though it presents an account of one man's thinking, the man is a ghost. No one besides the author knows him. No sources exist that prove he's a good man. The thinking is potential thinking. Every man reading it can say, "No, not me." Plus, wading into an explanation can be fiction suicide.

When it comes to oral histories, however, the self-censorship is endless. Alexievich describes:

If, for instance, besides the storyteller, there was some family member or friend in the apartment, or a neighbor (especially a man), she would be less candid and confiding than if it was just the two of us. It would be a conversation for the public. For an audience. That would make it impossible to break

through to her personal impressions; I would imme-
diately discover strong inner defenses. Self-control.
Constant correction. And a pattern even emerged:
the more listeners, the more passionless and ster-
ile the account. To make it suit the stereotype. The
dreadful would look grand, and the incomprehen-
sible and obscure in a human being would be in-
stantly explained. I would find myself in a desert
of the past, filled with nothing but monuments. (88)

When women expologize, they lean in to stereotype
and expectation, say what others want to hear. They
copy the newspapers' headlines or otherwise provide the newspapers with their headlines. For people
to know what is unique about her, what she wants
people to understand, they must first accept her expologies, which they do only when the expologies
hint at what is already established, fashionable, or
politically correct.

*

The disclaimer epidemic is even worse in the classroom. When women's nonfiction thoughts spill out,
a disclaimer usually follows. I have noticed only
women say things like: ". . . but I don't know what
you guys think" after communicating intelligent,
though maybe wonky-on-the-delivery, ideas. Female
students look to others to substantiate their ideas
with agreement. They give themselves a way out of
having to come up with a rebuttal if others do not
agree. They cast their thoughts as silly because silly

thoughts do not require backing. They retreat quickly. Others always win.

A friend who teaches English at a high school in Slovakia tells me, "We always end up taking boys to the regional competition because even though the girls speak better English, they lack in confidence."

How do educators teach female students not to expologize without targeting them as weaker, less confident individuals?

From the ground . . .

. . . by teaching girls at a young age that expologizing is not the answer. That we strive to be balanced individuals, not simply nice, kind, and selfless. By teaching girls they are autonomous human beings. Their thoughts, concerns, and ideas matter.

But even with a promising start, a woman's confidence teeters through puberty, hinging on any number of rejections from romantic interests. Most growing up happens outside middle school and high school classrooms. The #nomorexpologies campaign recruits mothers, fathers, sisters, brothers, friends, partners, and anyone else in a young woman's life to fight against indecision. It's everyone's problem.

up . . .

. . . by addressing it at the beginning of the semester. By saying all opinions matter and meaning it. Asking less of apologies and explanations and more of the core ideas students are trying to communicate. Formulating a pedagogy against apology that extends beyond written assignments into classroom etiquette: trusting that students use their phones only in an emergency, trusting that students are late because of unforeseen circumstances, and ultimately, trusting that students care about the subject at hand. After all, an adult student's presence in the college classroom should be foreshadowed by a desire to pursue one's education and career without a parent's prodding.

Ben Lerner, in a poem about the Academy featured in *No Art*, says, "As a policy, / we are generally sorry. But sorry doesn't cut it. / We must ask you to remove your shoes, your lenses, your teeth. / We must ask you to sob openly" (11). It is important for educators to turn this sobbing policy around. The Academy and millions of students depend on it.

*

Readers—and society as a whole—are as much to blame as writers. Instead of jumping the gun on critiquing a work of nonfiction, readers need to understand that even when a writer conducts a thorough investigation on a particular subject, one may leave some nooks and crannies undiscovered, especially when the subject is a person's entire lifetime or a country-wide initiative. If a reader knows better, having grown up in a particular cranny and weeded the garden there, one should begin a conversation with the author, the publisher, and the public to add to the pool of knowledge. Knowledge is collective. People create it through constant collaboration with others. Talking considerately and listening without being prompted would prevent women from prematurely asking for forgiveness or playing off a well-informed perception as a hunch no one needs to take seriously.

To participate in cultivating a community of women writers who don't expologize, it is necessary to:

1.   Acknowledge a writer's human incapacity to know absolutely everything there is to know, while staying cognizant of what may be missing from a particular work. And then talk. Always in this order. Understanding weakness leads to compassion in conversation. With this comes trusting women. They do as much as anyone to prepare and edit their nonfiction.

2.   Accept that predictions go awry. Suggestions that hold water now may spill in the future and not even hint at ever being contained. Adichie's apology is personal. "I'm sorry if this doesn't work out." But it does something for the public, too. It says, "Don't hold me accountable for something that happens in the future based on suggestions I make now." With this comes trusting women. Their guesses are educated.

3.   Let things be new and unidentifiable. Women writers like Svetlana and Mullally should not have to confirm what a book is and what it is not. They should not have to deem anything "purposeful." With this comes trusting women. They are experienced inventors, and their inventions are brilliant, credible tools.

Readers must refrain from tracking what's politically correct and what isn't. Writers who mean well should not be crucified. "Meaning well" is a subjective qualifier, but subjectivity isn't always a bad thing. It requires a thinking, feeling human being to make the call. Writers who are part of a movement and write to further the movement most likely mean well when it comes to that movement. Writers who write introductions describing the efforts undertaken to create a book most likely mean well when it comes to that book. Every woman writer whose words I scrutinize expologizes for a sincere reason: to fill the unknown with a cushion onto which dust can settle until perforated by an ass, or until the unknown becomes known.

Then there are the readers who are also writers who tend to police other writers if only to produce more liberally minded content and further their own careers. They do not always seek to have rational conversations, nor do they actively attempt to change the receiving end of their criticism. I'm guilty of it, too. In fact, calling out some of my favorite women writers for expologizing, which might qualify them as un-feminist, might be seen as exactly the kind of thing I'm talking about. But my aim in writing this is to start conversations not fights. I do not say, "They are bad feminists for expologizing."

The problem is this: it is easier to see that writers mean well when they expologize. If they do not (because they do not feel the need to expologize or because they aren't aware of the holes in their work, which is often the case), it is more difficult to tell. In other words, expologies soften the reader to the work. Oftentimes, they soften the reader enough that one is willing to forgive everything. So how can readers accurately judge a writer's intention without the presence of expologies? Should they trust that all women writers mean well? Or is it more nuanced than that? I do not have the answer.

A friend reads the bare bones of the examples I present and says, "I still see the above disclaimers as necessary and do not clearly see what is apologetic about them." I explain again and again why I see them as expologies. I figure he's trying to infuriate me. Sometimes when we read together, we purposelessly put each other down. If I say, "This writer writes like me," he will read one line and say, "I don't see it." I will tell him he has to "be there" as if the book and my voice have convened in a location he's staring at on a postcard. If he likes a particular image, such as that of a mother sweating her baby out from her pores, I will tell him I don't. I will tell him the image has actually become, sort of, cliché. In the end, I come to understand he's serious about not seeing the expologies, and I begin to wonder whether it's because they really aren't there or because he's a man.

*

What all of this leads to is not a campaign to completely stop women writers from expologizing, but to lessen how often they expologize and how they phrase their expologies. *In Men Explain Things to Me*, Solnit makes two great points:

I've learned that a certain amount of self-doubt is a good tool for correcting, understanding, listening, and progressing—though too much is paralyzing, and total self-confidence produces arrogant idiots. There's a happy medium between these poles to which the genders have been pushed, a warm equatorial belt of give and take where we should all meet. (5).

In this quote, Solnit affirms that expologies may be necessary ("a certain amount of self-doubt"), but that overdoing it on the expologies may be disastrous ("too much is paralyzing"). It is up to the writer to strike a balance between the two, critically unfolding the binary into other possibilities.

Solnit's second point is this: "We know less when we erroneously think we know than when we recognize that we don't. Sometimes I think these pretenses at authoritative knowledge are failures of language:

the language of bold assertion is simpler, less taxing, than the language of nuance and ambiguity and speculation" (82). While this quote also suggests that expologies are great communication tools, it mentions the words "nuance," "ambiguity," and "speculation," which expologies destroy. When a text is explained (this book is this, *not* this), it rids the work of these three magical species.

Solnit defends expologies because she also expologizes: "For the record, I do believe that women have explained things in patronizing ways, to men among others. But that's not indicative of the massive power differential that takes far more sinister forms as well or of the broad patterns of how gender works in our society" (13). In the paragraphs preceding this quote, Solnit incriminates men for overexplaining matters they may not fully understand. She includes a "for the record" to appease critics who may want to incriminate women in the same way, evening the playing field. She says, women overexplain too. I say, men also expologize.

It is important for women writers to acknowledge places where they may have been ignorant, but only when the text calls for it. Women writers have to treat expology like painting, which takes patience. If expology were indeed a game of ring toss, it would call for a single ring and a single target. If expology were another way to incentivize collective knowledge, it would read more like the end of a peer-reviewed article, suggesting further avenues to explore, and less like a sweeping edit, undermining the work.

As for readers, it is important for them to stay sharp, but also to yield to compassion. To not expect nor accept gratuitous expologies.

Women tend to apologize. I, a woman and a writer, resolve to change that.

Sources:

Adichie, Chimamanda Ngozi. *"The danger of a single story."* TED Global 2009.

Adichie, Chimamanda Ngozi. *Dear Ijeawele: a Feminist Mani festo in Fifteen Suggestions*. 4th Estate, 2018.

Alexievich, Svetlana. *The Unwomanly Face of War*. Penguin Books Ltd., 2018.

Lerner, Ben. *No Art*. Granta, 2016.

Mullally, Una. *Repeal the 8th*. Unbound, 2018.

Solnit, Rebecca. *Men Explain Things to Me: And Other Essays*. Granta, 2014.

A child's eyes light up at the sight of a playground, a cityful of entertainment. It is raining sporadically, the sky's blue-bruised skin healing to reveal blooming white. You prepare to shut your book at any moment; your thumb, serving as an interactive bookmark, starts to swell with pain. Does your phone really reach vulnerable cells in your head? You glance up and startle: the building is SPLIT

IN HALF, even though you have been here for years. What injury does it mime? The sky inside is a woman's inside. The air, the wind, and the rain penetrate her. Have you closed your eyes while opening your mouth to a gloved hand? Drank the droplets a dog shook off its back as if they were as natural and nutritious as flakes of fresh snow?

You wonder who leaves the *or* in clitoris for other women to find. A sign that says: your pleasure is not guaranteed. For men to not find the clitoris, as if it were somewhere different each time, like a set of keys. Some women learn how to die and only then how to live. After a time, they endorse clit *and* is (co-existence goddess: I could not stop her from giving birth to herself if I tried). They grow up to be strong women who lend rest / room thoughts and emails with news from your home country. They say you're strong, too, even though you delay writing about the underside of *some women* till winter when snow is the visible underside of heaven. A heaven that's learning how to die.

Yours was the first but not only female body you have loved. As a way to the female brain, to her soul. Because your eroticism has always been stronger than friendship. Eroticism leads to just as leads to eroticism.

You teach your eight-year-old cousin how to shave her legs in a blue plastic tub. You don't want to be alone in your family's *body of a young woman*—every family has one, dictates what she can eat, can wear, where she can go, can come. Seven hours later your cousin is nineteen and an au pair in America, so you're not alone in *this* body either, the body of a migrant, bilingual, an accent coming up the throat like vomit. Your grandmother slaps the razor out of her hand and spills the bricked driveway, yelling something you don't remember years later, making this a scene out of a silent film. She and your mother are both bodies of mothers. The hair grows back thicker. Your catharsis when the legs grow back stronger.

On your twenty-fourth January, you wear lingerie under your overalls and appreciate a body that can conduct its own train and round the bend. It feels sturdy in its conductivity. It is conducive to knowing and getting what it needs: instead of men who protect her, men who protect themselves, instead of men who treat a woman's body like a beached whale getting her wet out of pity, men who plan her orgasms on Google Calendar. A body that isn't conducive to knowing what it needs (like you at eighteen) acts like a toddler who repeatedly yells, "I want to do this by myself," yet looks around for anyone willing to tell her the rules.

You break your first line of poetry before your first heart. The first time you break a body you're too dry, and this isn't really you but the girl he dates after you who sends him to the emergency room clutching an intestinal worm smelling of dick. For some reason, at first, you blame her. Then he learns to slow down, copying the rhythmic sounds of household items: a coffee machine gurgling, a chair being dragged up, then placed back, a piece of toast sinking into silver, then popping out. Printer-pace. How it first pulls the paper through, like a thread through a needle, then for a short time speeds up to print the words, before gently letting go, like a kiss. You hack his computer to type a single line, wanting to feel the extra-long buttery swoosh.

The paper jams.

He's above you heavening, but it's you who's heaving. Suddenly, you're swiping a tarot deck from the thrift store, wanting to confirm this is neither a time nor a place. You might have ovulated this month, but you don't know. Thirty percent off your most expensive item, so you want to sell them your egg. Good price, good price, you elbow the counter. You're unsure of how tarot works, but you're sure the fear of possessing it isn't helping. You don't really believe in things, but you don't not believe in them either. You call your extent of believing "reading into." Like condoms. You read into their ability to protect you from fetuses flying at the speed of unmanned tennis balls. In middle school, someone teaches you to fill the condom with water to check it for holes—a belly-full piglet. Now you read so much pro-life media that you start seeing the fetuses (clumped at the bottom like sand) wave at you with banjo-hands. That same night, your back's in a draught. A sticky film dries like sea salt. When you move, you crack open like an egg. The film crumbles onto the Man of Wands and gives it away: he came in your past. The statute of limitations for pregnancy has passed.

Long after you learn you will most definitely get pregnant if you have sex, you learn you can only get pregnant at a certain time of month. You think it's a trick. After the horror stories and maximum-security education and DVR recordings of *16 and Pregnant*, a rumor changes sex forever. The rumor is calendarific. It is ovulatory. It is about patience and counting cards. If you wait, hold his erection by a string, like a carrot on a stick, you won't blow up.

All gods have a name but God. All moons have a name but the moon. All babies have a name but Baby. Anonymous wraps around his dick; does it matter if it's a mouth or vagina? You once told a man you were dating that he was interchangeable—kind, easily humored. You didn't hear the end of it for a week, and you liked hearing the end of it. I love you. You're welcome. Do most fathers thank women for giving birth to their children? When they hold their hands and say prayers on each finger, a rosary bodied. When they smell the warmth of delivery, the feces, the iron of blood. When they cannot help but contract their urethras because for once their dicks are smaller than the vagina that is happening in the room.

Trevor Noah does a skit about the power of the vagina. He thanks the vagina by talking about it. The audience thanks the vagina by laughing. By laughing, they talk about it. At Costco, people eat bite-sized samples of adult foods before assuring the cameras they can afford them. But it's members-only. Everyone else must not know how to get one. A woman. They need to be taken seriously. They need to be serious to be taken lightly. "To be taken," take her, take her away. "How do you take your coffee?" "Woman."

Women are allowed to say things during pregnancy that normally they can only say on their periods. Anything can be said about pregnancy since the only people who feel it only feel it. Being pregnant is like walking home from the party of your life; your ride is whiny and aloof. He shows up later, asking you to congratulate him for having a birthday, even though it's you who made him and his gifts. Comparatively, the table is pregnant with your half-sipped coffee and half-daydreams waiting to interrupt. You are the bystander owner of these items, meaning you are the father. Focused, you stop listening. Having nothing is better than lukewarm imagination, lukewarm freedom.

The cell phones have built-in toothaches.
Because each tooth is wired to a key, each word results in a different kind of ache. M-O-T-H-E-R, B-A-B-Y. F-U-R-T-H-E-R is the most painful because of "u," because of the second "r." It accents the pain found in F-A-T-H-E-R. When you refuse to go any further, the pain washes out.

His roommate's dog eats your blood out of the garbage can and spreads it over the carpet like jelly. The party's leftovers. Licks of tape left over from birthday streamers. Your excrement becomes part of the landscape: Western, locatable. A GPS coordinate on your punctuation. "Uhm can you tell your girlfriend to stop leaving tampons in the bathroom," to use whiteout on her water, to erase her progeny / somewhere else?

Blood is excretion, is extract. He asks you, "You consider blood . . ." an excerpt of your condition? "Oh, right, you're a woman. For you, it's like shit. It doesn't automatically mean violence." In truth, you excrete blood out of your eyeball, wear a patch twice a month for good measure. Once when the blood actually flows and once when a clear film is ready to birth life, something like tears. It's true. You cry when over-stimulated, physically or emotionally. When a man says, "Let me please you, you deserve it, you don't have to love me back," all you hear are contingencies.

You look for clues to a crime in a series of crimes, a serial kinkiness. Except your intentions are to do the opposite: to *decriminalize* kink. On a boat in Copenhagen, a couple talks about someone they know having gotten whipped at a bachelor party in front of his bride. The lapping waves slapping the boat imitate the whip's kiss. Would you do it? Would *you*? A clue. Later, in a stranger's home, you find books about sex work. They stand out like watermelons in a tomato patch—the deep red of guts, the green of the unripe. You underline Maggie Nelson's *Argonauts* because it is ridden, bed-ridden. The pencil lines you make are the platforms found in aquariums where giant fish do tricks. You want to convince your partner to publish erotic poetry he wrote only for you because it would clue him in to a fearless, destigmatized sexuality. "Does sexuality have to be public to be fearless?" It's the only definition of fearless you know.

The bachelor chooses the woman who wants to be a mother over the woman who orders a bouncy castle and rides him in a flesh-pink bikini. The woman who wants to be a mother watches the woman who orders a bouncy castle and rides him in a flesh-pink bikini hang on him like a monkey on the blowy purple floor. From her moral high ground, she says, "She pounced on him like a piece of meat, and I'm like hmm . . . what is happening here." The woman he doesn't choose becomes the butt of the joke. The joke is the entire season, the whole show.

The Bachelor hires you as the *you are here* sticker. They hire the map of California as the map. The job description reads, *Remind people which reality they're on*. They tend to forget, always having to confess their reality.

"You mean, remind them they're on *The Bachelor*, not, say, *Survivor*?"

"Exactly."

As a Catholic, you go to confession. As a Catholic woman, you're set behind the foreground of the man hearing your confession. As a Catholic woman who's also a writer, you're reminded there's no one reminding you which reality you're on every time you stand up from your desk.

"Each year, Friday evening of the conference features *Breaking Silences: An Abortion Speak Out.* This is a space for people who have had abortions to share their stories in a safe and supportive environment. Listening to such personal stories frames the weekend and grounds conference conversations in lived experiences."

(Hampshire College, Amherst, MA)

Women cheer because their voices are being heard. They are not cheering for abortion itself. People who are pro-choice aren't "for abortion."

Why do they cheer?
Their voices are being heard.

Why are their voices being heard?
Because they cheer.
Because they have had an abortion.

But, *his* logic:

Why have they had an abortion?
Because their voices are being heard.

He is pro-choice in theory. But in practice? His friends. They come crawling out of their reproductive cubbyholes. Since giving birth to him, as friends do by showing you to yourself, they have grown. The sea has spawned waves he never dreamed were possible from shore. They hit the deck, clapping.

               "That's just my humble opinion."
"I thought it was a memory?"
               "That's just my humble memory."

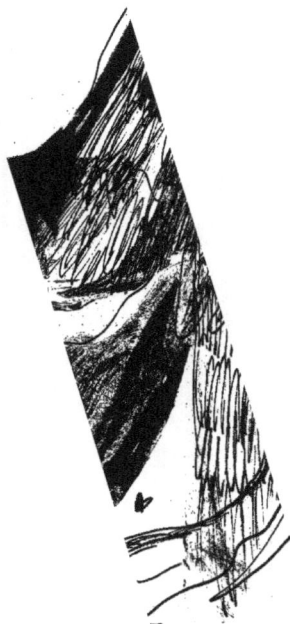

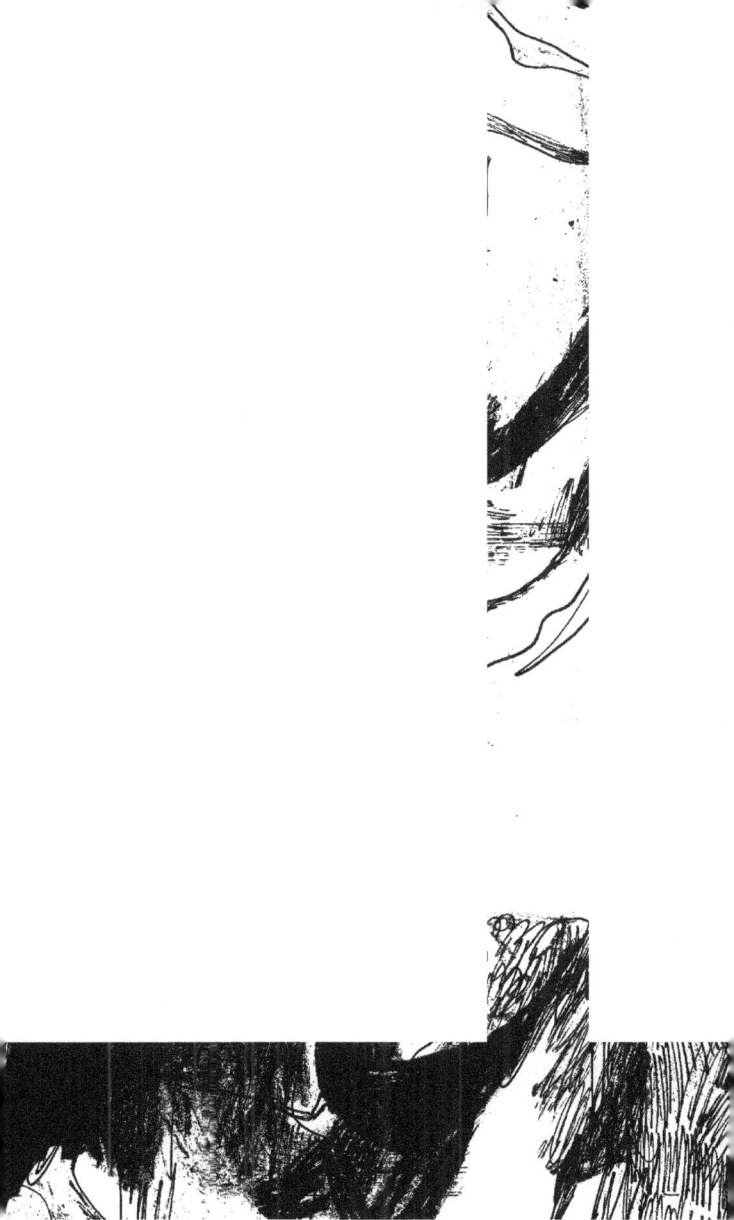

I posted on the "official English language subreddit for Poland," asking people for their opinions on Poland's abortion laws and experiences at The Black Protest(s). Among my questions were: what's it like to live in your body? Who's responsible for your suffering? If you could live anywhere in the world, where would you live and why? Here are some of the responses, taken verbatim from the post. I limited my editing to spelling and major grammar errors in order to preserve the feeling of this digital room. Bracketed material has been added by me for the sake of coherence.

Doctors are scared to give this recommendation or perform the procedure because of political pressure.

The doctor [Chazan, 2014] had backing from Radio Maryja as he is their made man.

It's controversy—it sells very well.

EDIT: Don't get me wrong. I support you, and I believe that you can be really scared because of the image the media has created.

And received another job, as a lecturer, afterwards. It's not like he's out.

Two *known* cases. There might have been others the media is unaware of.

Two cases are two too many in a civilized country.

Believe me, I had enough experience with shitty doctors . . . Poland is an awful place to have a baby.

It's easier for victims to get damages when it's loud about medical wrongdoings.

The doctors have a sanction to use the conscience clause above medical knowledge.

And yeah, he was painted as a hero by rightwing media because . . . guess what! . . . they are rightwing media! When it comes to the leftwing media, he was painted as a charlatan. It's pretty obvious that the right will treat him as a hero, and the left will treat him as an imbecile—it's all about ideology

. . .

Right-wing media is a mouthpiece for the government.

Ergo (the word I think you don't understand).

Goverment is actually spelled government. You can remember it by n before the m. Have a nice day!

Most people in Poland are alright with the current laws regarding abortion, which have been present since 1993, and don't want them to change—neither into more restrictive ones, nor into less restrictive ones.

If I had to choose, however, I would loosen them rather than tighten.

I would have attended the Black Protest; however, I no longer live in Poland.

Recognizing that abortion is a sensitive issue, and

that people can hold good-faith views on all sides,
I believe that government should be kept out of
the matter, leaving the question to each person for
one's conscientious consideration.

Abortion is brought up whenever the government
wants to divert society's attention from other sensitive topics. It also helps enforce the "we" versus
"them" divide that devours and weakens our nation
since the Smolensk tragedy [2010 plane crash that
killed many members of the Polish government,
including the president and his wife].

I have attended all Black Protests in Poland. I am
also sick of hearing about the subject in the media
and from politicians who talk about it to cover up
other stuff. I believe that better sexual education
will lead to less abortions.

EDIT: we need to be realistic. There's no possibility right now to have no crimes committed in our
country. We can only try to minimize that number,
but we also need to acknowledge the fact that the
situation is not as bad as media tells us it is.

Although I will move out to Norway. I've got
education, and I am sick of our current situation in
Poland.

Those who can—do—and those who cannot—teach.

I'm female and living in Poland. I support the Black Protest. However, my friends and family are highly religious, so I don't feel comfortable being open about it.

(deleted)

I'm actually in a lesbian relationship right now, so at least I don't have to worry about the government stripping me of my reproductive rights unless someone decides to rape me.

No church wedding for *Babcia's* [grandma's] sake? ;)

Not because they are believers. The main argument is "not worth the drama," or the eternal "for *babcia's* / parents' sake" or "this is the tradition."

Many Poles are ritual Christians.

Especially in most corpo-worlds being gay is better than being straight cuz muh diversity.

Oh boohoo.

And same-sex marriage doesn't mean shit in a country where most heterosexual couples don't bother to marry at all. Just go live with ur partner and enjoy life instead of letting stupid politics consume your mind constantly.

My wife is British-Chinese, and surprisingly the place she feels most comfortable and relaxed in public is Poland.

Kinda funny that this "racist" little country of Poland is the place where we feel safest and most accepted in a strange, cold Polish way.

Unfortunately, a lot of our society is backwards.

"I will call people 'backwards' because they do not agree with my opinion that being promiscuous and irresponsible is the way to go."

Dialogue is reciprocal or non-existent.

"Other people having sex is my problem."

This opinion is deeply rooted in religious bullshit ("sex is sin," "sex is for procreation only," "accept God's will," "you must carry your cross," etc.).

In LTRs [long-term relationships], it's EXTREMELY unlikely to have unwanted pregnancy IF all the safety measures are followed. It's like demanding laws that protect you from getting flunked at school. Play it by the book, and you'll be alright.

Not spreading your legs during your couple fertile days plus the lifecycle of the sperm does prevent pregnancy 100%.

Who are you (or who is the government) to tell adults when they should and shouldn't "spread their legs"?

Your freedom ends where another person's freedom begins.

The problem with extremely permissive abortion laws is, first off, men would be at women's mercy when it comes to casual sexual relationships and their repercussions. And second off, it would chiefly be used by promiscuous lower-class women as an emergency exit rather than women who fall in the category of special cases that are not included in the current legislation.

(Actually, I can't think of any reason other than to have a backup plan in case of failed slutting.)

I guess the best country that is the least far from home is Germany. It's historically ironic, but I'd probably get better treatment there than in my own country. My favorite university professor, an expert in his field, is actually leaving for Germany after this academic year ends because he's fed up with the direction this country is headed. He's gotten married to a dude (on German soil, of course), and I guess he wants to live in a society that respects him.

If I could, I would live in Australia just for the lack of extreme weather disasters.

Freedom is not just a permission to act.

Our abortion laws are backwards, as is, for instance, the new law that requires stores to be closed on Sundays.

Obviously bad analogy is obvious.

For the sake of consistency, in many western countries shops are closed on Sundays (including Belgium).

We (women in Poland) in majority have brains and bodies, so we can think about consequences before we use our body.

What suffering?

I am disabled with chronic back pain due to repeated malpractice when handling my condition in my youth. My current doctors tell me it's about 70% chance I will be able to carry a pregnancy to term without ending up in a wheelchair. I would love to take this chance; however, I need to have the option to terminate if my health so dictates. I cannot be sure this will be respected in Poland. In fact, I suspect it won't be. And it's not just abortion. Even if I carry the baby in full, I can only give birth via caesarian due to my hips being deformed as well. However, I read of women who were forced to give birth naturally, even with tons of medical documentation advising against. If I give birth naturally, I will not walk again. That's 100%. Again, another medical matter I'm not sure will be taken into account. I want a child very badly, but I'm terrified to have one in this country. Fortunately, my parents-in-law are in the UK, and they can afford to provide care for me. If things don't change in the next couple of years, I will just go there for the duration of my pregnancy. This will likely mean going through most of it without my mother and my partner, but if this is the sacrifice I have to make to be treated like a human being, I will make it.

There are obvious reasons why we limit personal freedoms in such cases, and none of them apply to abortion.

It is outstanding, and hilarious, that it is the women that are mainly pro-abortion, which shows them being far less sensitive and more materialistic than they should be, or at least that's what I think. In [It is] very unlike the fair gender of female.

Be a woman is like to be a man, and it's much better than to be an unborn.

Living here as a woman is scary, not that I feel it on an everyday basis, but it gets scary real quick when I think about it. (So I try not to.)

Existance is actually spelled existence. You can remember it by ends with -ence. Have a nice day!

So?

New throwaway account asking about a hot topic that is very likely to cause a shitstorm?

Nope, nothing, don't pay attention to the man behind the curtain.

a timeline

On April 15, 2018 you post on Reddit. "What suffering?" "I love my country, but people are trying to Westernize it. I assume 'you' are one of those hateful people.' A hateful person puts his country, his blood, on a map and hangs it in a lecture hall for intellectuals to slam their thoughts against it. A hateful person puts his country's blood up for adoption. Using the internet, the commenter is Western; attempting to reach him, you are Eastern. You have sewn your pride to a white flag, a dull red nipple dipped in its own milk. You have agreed not to defend Poland from the east; you have agreed not to defend Poland from the East. Instead, you swipe the sun from the conveyor belt in the West to stop placental colors from dripping into his veins. You impose an embargo on warm visions.

As a child, you sink your friend's sunsets in a bucket of water, convincing her it's all the rage in art—colors made to run blurry, like heat waves on asphalt.

You used to think time zones got it wrong. The United States should be leading other countries to (vi)c(to)ry. You took your grandmother for lagging. Then time shaped your immigrant perception of time. On asphalt, you are (s)p(o)iled sky while your friends look like sunsets in photographs. Now you what rhymes with sky.

> On October 3, 2016 operating eight hours behind Poland, you're nostalgic for time because of difference in no / ws. "It is natural, human, to long for the past, particularly when we can remember our histories better than they were" (Roxane Gay, *Bad Feminist*). Having immigrated to the West, of course you remember history better than it was. You meet history after it's had time to learn the rules and practice.
>
> America kills to be new.

On January 4, 2017 the Vatican tweets: *tears of a mother's pain become seeds of life and hope.* And you think, if suffering makes a woman fertile, then happiness must carve out her womb and hang it, dripping, in the barn—spoils of a never-ending war. And then she must beg the cross noose around her neck to reunite her with her memory, her smile wiped up like a spill. It is only when she has cried enough seeds to replenish the Garden of Eden that she has suffered enough.

Hope exists in the head, the heart, or "the holy," says a man with a PhD in hope. A woman with a pained expression operates a brightly colored choo-choo in front of Forever XXI. Your friend whispers, "At least she's warm." "I beg your pardon?" The eggs.

Politicians who *fight for life* are really fighting for a woman's pain to fight for life. At least she's war / m and the Vatican honest.

"And some historians said that war was an extension of political action, while others disagreed and said that on the contrary, political action was a continuation of war and anyway war never ended but was simply transformed and assumed a different form."

(Patrik Ouředník, *Europeana*)

Who knew you were going to (say) war.

On January 16, 2017 you read someone the tweet, and she says, "In some ways it's true." You take a disgusted bite of your banana-yellow eggs and ask about tears of joy. Do they exist. Do they mean death and the opposite of hope. Anticipation is educated hope, and an educated guess is the opposite of guessing. If an orgasm is a little death—*la petite mort*—then maybe laughter is, too. In another conversation, are you genuinely pro-choice? He asks your memory, which refuses to admit your once neutrality. Born Catholic implies your parents never had sex, and this makes you invincible. But women are forced into sex forced into pregnancy. Women consent to sex are forced into pregnancy. Women consent to sex consent to pregnancy and still lament over the coffee they left outside their pregnancy. It's less taxing to doubt whether someone loves you than whether you are capable of love.

In August 2018, in Ireland, you read *proper Catholic burial* and wonder why Catholicism isn't more creative. Bless the child in the womb. Vote the second coming into existence. Sometimes, women consent to unprotected sex because they are afraid of disappointing the men who demand it. "But is it utopia we're fighting for?" he asks. Do men consent to protecting their children because they are afraid of disappointing the women who demand it? Make it about something other than sacrifice. Sacrifice is glorified quitting. You sacrifice the Pope by accident—you reserve tickets, then change your plans. You fly to the U.K. instead, looking for them at the airport. Victims. Abortion tourism: is the glass half full or empty with *the right to travel?*

She is a woman's purse, full of useless things: an artist's ability to draw / conclusions, *staircase* wit. Late-
ly, her cervix has been lying to her—*I'm at work.*[3]
Humans are breakable machines. A little heat, a little
grease. Sometimes they need to be replaced altogeth-
er by babies that don't feel misanthropy at catchy
tunes and alliteration. Ghost vessels and tumors are
deceptive ghosts, pre- the real thing: vessels and
death. When you wear contacts, trying to improve
your contact with the world, your eyes grow ghosts
to suck up more oxygen; if they fill with blood, expel
ghost, you'll go blind. He wears red boxers to support the cause, their smile rising above his pants. "I
was supposed to wear red, but I figured my period
counts." Does a mouth reading *vagina* to a roomful
of chewing strangers, popping thought bubbles like
an indecisive cartoonist? "You're fine in the presence
of a crocheted uterus," but you can't ask to carry it
as a synecdochical shadow. She puts her head on
your shoulder, whispers *thank you* months after you
have nothing to do with her country's leaving Poland
to fend for itself.

[3] In Ireland, hundreds of women developed cervical cancer after having a misdiagnosed CervicalCheck smear test. Once the
mistake was realized, responsibility was thrown around, and no
one notified the women affected. The scandal came to light when
Vicky Phelan, one of the women affected, discovered she was giv-
en incorrect smear test results; after winning a court case against
the lab, she refused to sign a "non-disclosure" agreement.

On December 12, 2016 you hear *exact ancestry* at a gathering of women and think *this isn't the way to remember.* Calling blood by a single name: anato / my. *Exact ancestry* doesn't account for all the names you naively give your future children; by naming them, you induct them to your ancestry. In elementary school you like the name Acey, but your friends see *air conditioner.* You speed through Derek, Lila, Miles, Oliver. It is only with one partner that you neglect to name a child, so that genealogy remains endless. All these children are not yet exact people. It is them you inherit. So your identity is fluid. Who you make will make you, the cruelest of karma.

You have since given up dating purebred Polish men or, for that matter, any man too certain of his (your) identity because children are capable of becoming women and starting wars.

This solves a lot of problems. A family history that's a blank canvas: a family understudy.

For your wish to be granted—to return to the women in the photographs who live with in / exact ancestry—you need to collect tears as unique as snowflakes. *Be careful what you wish for.* You look over your wish like an exam. You store the tears in a deep, cool well to prevent them from spoiling. Your hands, having multiplied to build the well, are the only structures visible from the outer reaches of your reaching out to Poland.

If you shake many globes, somewhere they will still have fallen by your hand.

You are window shopping politics

when you surprise yourself with tears. You gawk at women who look like you and wonder why you have more compassion for them than anyone else. It must be that compassion grows with distance and duration. The farther the object of compassion, the longer you have not *been* the object, the more intense the feeling. To see resemblance in a mannequin is a privilege. You touch yourself to remember you are not made of plastic the color of a crater.

You watch backyard birds munch on grassed debris at the speed of highway lanes in troubled rain. You can't tell whether anything's in their mouth. And then you can: a dandelion's tail, a witch's wig. The ball could be under any one of the cups. They fast / forward when everything around stays the same.

Or does compassion grow with loyalty to blood, ancestry, borders, and wars. You recognize Polish bone structure from a mile away, you tell your father. He laughs. You hug furniture to your chest in order to remove yourself from assigning seats simply because they're there (they're no longer there).

You are the musical chair.

On January 24, 2017 you finally put it together. You do it in a classroom full of people missing their activism because it passes faster than their education. *Objects in mirror are closer than they appear.* People move too slowly for a lifetime. They need a second life seven or eight hours behind, but sometimes even that doesn't cut it. By writing about the protest you miss, you're documenting a truth removed from experience. And history. Unless history meets you on the other side of the ocean where you're invested in living (instead of living) and collecting the moment to someday moment the collection. Around you, people have sunk into their phones, thinking this is a protest is a protest is a protest. Maybe someday someone will thank you for brushing away the hair from a spot on the neck that tempts sweetly with blood swimming just underneath the skin. But you wouldn't bet on it. You're being selfish. Remember you gave him Jewish.

You take a lesson in the head, feel for thousands of time.

If an orgasm is a natural human victory,

you have agreed not to run blurry like . . .

        politicians who look like heat waves on as-
phalt.

Your hands keep multiplying to count their legs

      up. Existence is pro-choice.

Passion is the place where we versus them

spoils.

You move to the East Coast and take a mile away

      another mile

          mile

Magnificent Mile

because you want nothing more than to reach them.

In September 2018, on the outskirts of Skopje, an afternoon stroll puts a caffeine crash to bed. As pavement turns to chalky rubble, you pick up walnut shells the texture of firewood—caves innervated with alphabets. While washing them in the outdoor artist's sink the bridge of one of the halves breaks off, the bridge between your logic and his when he tries to wash you of your thoughts. Immediately *the other* is cancerous. From this stems a poor desire: to sculpt a walnut woman overrun with tumors. Writing can depict an idea without your eyes. You do not have to exercise it (exorcise it).

The sun is an orgy on two fronts: one of lack, the other of abundance.

You listen to an interview with a woman deported to Mexico who was forced to leave her three children a. behind or b. in front of her in the United States. Woman deported or deported woman, can a person become irreversibly attached to an adjective? When becoming a state. *A liquid conforms to its container.* Her eldest daughter did not like to visit because when she did, with her baby, she a. stayed for months at a time or b. bypassed physics. The laws of the universe. *A liquid confirms to its...* grandma comfort. Then the woman cooked and cooked, but they didn't come. Temporary forgiveness impedes dailiness unbothered. Babies do not haunt their mothers in fear of being loved too much. A storage room sits a. full of empty boxes, b. full of space.

You print pictures without thinking about the pockets they create in the unseen world. Until you do. Then the walls are too white behind paintings. Too often paintings of women are exits for attention. The mind invariably turns to the woman, turns *on* the woman. Each preposition opens a new door, a new meaning. Go ahead, enact every preposition on a woman: *with* a woman, *through* her. She will only love you if you talk her out of her opinion. The standard of opinion is love.

On April 18, 2018, you correct everyone, *the pilot was a woman*. But no one can fathom a woman would have that much control. She did what she had to do; she landed the plane. And you wonder if she was scared, if she pictured the passengers as plastic dolls, unable to be hurt by a bad performance, rather than as an audience divorced from their undergarments, able to provide a laugh and maybe abate embarrassment. "They give senile women rubber baby dolls at old people's homes and the residents rock them for hours, anesthetizing themselves with the rhythm." (Dubravka Ugresic, *The Fox*). When you are first learning to drive, you pretend every car is a cloud, a large wad of cotton. Your Mother scolds you for being dangerous, so you switch back. You strip the drivers their opaque, meaty skin turning red, green, like a dizzying, expensive fountain, but this does not ease your nerves. Since one looks too long at the color stop, how much training does it take to reverse the effect?

His old babysitter used to count to one hundred when she drove. He asks you to count to one hundred and to make it to your destination before you reach the apex. This is a weird game, you think, against *yourself*. Your refusal slows down time, stunts the poor child's growth. Each time you say "no," you remove a bus stop from his route to paradise. You feel uncomfortable with the sudden silence when the dishwasher stops. Glow-in-the-dark vengeance.

Reading outside, you're confronted with a rotten wood smell that's actually a lawn being sprayed with parmesan. The yellow wicker chair collects goose shit and packages, while the doctor's no longer your lover, and your sanity's no longer sanitary.

Your roommate never turns off her radio, even after she leaves. You keep mistaking it for voices inside your head.

On September 25, 2017, sleeping alone for the first time in days, you lie awake and wonder about love. How it digests. Is your new love, stuffed with time, just materialism? Possession disguised as desire limits your partner to being available to others only through quotes / marks. You're a sanitary heterosexual couple. You don't want to name your relationship, but you're inevitably advancing towards names and marriage. You read Maggie Nelson's *Argonauts* and take away end goals. Now it's night two, and there's a whole dance you do to prevent the end goal. Your coupledom's number one fan is a slick bottle of medical sanitizer posted on the nightstand. All of your partners have respected your decision to do away with eating hormones as a form of *control*, which says a lot about your ability to choose. The same can't be said for your college roommates who ganged up on you like a herd of stampeding advertisements, and now they're diving out of airplanes and getting engaged among parachutes breathing hard last breaths, oblivious to all the times they made you cry. Miniscule pushback on the #1 fan. It has the potential to blow your genitals' capabilities way out of proportion.

Sometimes all you want to do in a poem is take a walk. Activist intentions clear under the flat of your boots. They're equipped to detect the state of the ground, like an anus is equipped to detect what it wants to release: solid, liquid, or gas. Nature's infinity being the single most believable truth means authenticity blooms even in arboretum. "We're flowing," he tells his parents, and you've never felt more bred into coupled singularity.

In November 2017, you sit on the porch in an unfamiliar part of the country. It's so green from the plane like magnifying a jar of pesto. What you feel in his parents' house is sharp, like music leaving high-definition speakers. Knick-knacks on the mantel are the old Compromise, and now you're living inside that problem. Over coffee, his mother tells you she gave birth to him on all fours, and you can't help but compare. While planning her trip to Budapest, pregnant with assumptions, you book an air-conditioned coach with spacey bathrooms. Between the two of you teeters responsibility for her son, who kneels behind you and depends on your teeth gnawing the clay sheets.

May 26, 2019, if your relationship had a birthday, this would be it. A combination of three of your exes were born on this day, so you celebrate their losses. Stories traverse a table the size of a road sign. It's tradition. Not to see a movie, but to see a terrible one. Not to order coffee, but to be disappointed. This birthday, you're in a house with foreign animals and prayers. You tag-team to clean up blood after a cat ping-pongs a mouse, half kills it in an uncommitted match, one creature clearly defenseless. You're arguing about the poetics of *fucking*: when it's OK and every other time when it's a surprise. This match is better. Maggie Nelson's *Bluets* is the cause of the conversation, but you wish you were privy to *why she wrote it*. If you acted on your evil impulses, like behaving horribly around his friends or stealing packages from cumulous porches, would you keep falling, perpetually? You plan to disguise your fragility with tattoo sleeves. Even holding a leash would look meaty. But he already knows, says, this is a hug for anxiety, for cold and sore lips, for a sleepless night, for persimmons, those persnickety comments.

Barbara Ann Kipper, author of *14,000 Things to Be Happy About*, might actually be sad. Everyone's a hypocrite. Sometimes feminism is so comfortable that it's harder to watch TV than get rid of victims by leaning on them until they tip over. Every relationship is a leash. And people don't mind as long as their owners remember to walk them. Teenagers with leg beef line up to eat.

On July 2, 2019, your parents fly to Poland without you. For an immigrant, the commute home is long; imagine that episode on House Hunters: *please, no farther than two in-flight meals and one layover.* You cry on your way to a man-made lake, the rows of shops you pass looking like wet matchboxes. You imagine the family's gathering in the bright yellow kitchen, your father and uncle ducking under the ceiling light as they make their way to the hallway fridge. At noon, as a "dinner" call for families across Poland, the radio will broadcast St. Mary's Trumpet Call, played in the highest tower of St. Mary's Cathedral in Kraków, once in each of the four cardinal directions. Friends sacrifice citrus in a quiet backyard bonfire and summon spirits in each of the four cardinal directions, too. How could you have known? The tune, magical, as if played in literature, makes you feel five again, circling your grandmother's rose on a pink bike and pointing at airplanes, saying, "My parents live there." In transit. Two days later, you're sitting at a baseball game, reading Lily Hoang and anticipating shots of color. You feel warm among Americans enjoying American things. Everyone has something to hide. A soap bubble ultimately splits on rock. A lip on lip.

In 2017, your grandmother plans to create jobs for Americans No, that's Trump. No, that's you. Your grandmother creates a job for you by believing what they say about Trump on the Polish news. You want to scream because you're such an immigrant, and she's even more of one, sleeping, dislocated, on the wired phone with her two immigrant children in the place she never left.

a folio of ancestors

A woman swallows the middle of birth only to spit out a grown woman's body. How astonished the doctors are that pregnancy is about the mother. You've known all along because the nurse read aloud the nutrition label on the placenta: the #1 ingredient was place. In the city, synthetic stars illuminate one's inauguration to bliss. The country, however, relies on peppermints to free its breath as one thrashes about in souring puddles of spilled milk. Knees burn against concrete, raising bishop's flower tears on the skin. An ant hill billows like a circus tent. There are too many rare diseases to be able to escape each one.

For the first few years of her marriage, your grandmother is a powerless apartment, knocking on doors with her bones. The doors lead to smaller and smaller bones. She begs your grandfather to be there for your mother's birth, but her begging is muffled by Germany's promise of money, like rain when a house grows tumors, erupts in veins carrying whispers along the hall. *Duty is the death of love.* When he returns, he moves his family (*her* duty) to his hometown where he swaps signatures for a plot of land. She spends over forty years in that valley where varieties of green moss blend like coffee beans. Church bells dong, chasing birds from the branches. At the open-air market, she spends worthless currency, her immigrant grandchild's hand more desirable than the fruit everyone fondles like a breast. Soon, every shop will be gleaming with cheap primary-colored lanterns, and the cemetery will light up, showing who is loved and who is too far gone. It's a map of landmines; love can blow (someone) up. Late summer, she pianos a path in the blue woods, collecting mushrooms. She teaches you all there is to know about picking. All she can about choosing.

You're returned to Poland like a doll with ripped seams. Writing nightly to a chorus of howling dogs increases your sensitivity to all the ways pain can be communicated. How do you know they aren't hurt? You invite in a lamp from another room whose shade you throw to the floor like a dress, to give the walls a sip of soft light. The next morning, you drive your grandmother to the train station down thin country roads and cannot comprehend that she's the one departing, for a funeral. As you wait for the train to arrive, she tells you her mother was a saint and begins to cry. Her father was buried alive at a construction site; she told you this when you were an anxious child having to confirm with anything breathing that you'd make it through the night—*there are worse things*. After his death, her mother took her six children in armfuls to the altar and asked God to give them a good life and education in exchange for her chastity. Her favorite brother lived in a children's home. Another kind of begging. A troublesome boy, one less mouth to feed. There, he learned how to ice skate and play chess, skills he eventually taught the children his mother kept. She, being the youngest (though she may not have been), never learned how to swim because her mother didn't trust her by the river with the boys. "I want only women to keep me safe," you tell your lover after you reluctantly pass a cop car and firetruck riddled with idle, laughing men on your walk. If you opened them, cheap desires would spill like hastily packed closets.

"Mother, what do you have in store for us?!" she interrogates her blood, throwing her arms to the heavens. Her cold, purple fingers dig out a crumpled handkerchief, unfold it, and press it to her baggy eyes. Tragedy has been striking her family chronologically—in descending birth order. She's prepared to grieve for her siblings and herself, wearing a gown tagged with objects from her childhood in the few places memory has made sticky. A hospital, a children's home—they were all ill-fitting. It was customary, when one entered, to do the sign of the birth:

father   *son*

Now she does the sign of the cross unevenly,

Father

         Son

grazing her skin simply to remind herself she's alive; pinching has long been too harsh of a souvenir brought back from the land of dreams. There God lends His body's furniture. He measures how fragile she is pressed against His bare chest, the itchy green sofa—will she fall through? like a reckless ice skater on a glass of land.

Two days later, you pick her up at 5am. You tell your grandfather you're setting your alarm for 4:30, and he thinks he's the alarm. Already awake by the rooster's call, he shouts your name up the stairs he can't climb. In the car, no matter what you try, the screen shouts *RADIO LOCKED*, which robs you of a meaningful dawn. Your attempt to get coffee from the vending machine is thwarted by *tap and pay*, a special feature you're shocked your American card doesn't have. Back at home, she persuades you to cleave the pines' lowest bits and set them ablaze. It's what keeps the trees healthy. "Mother, no matter what, the young grow." The lampshade watches over the brightness expanding.

These notes are for her. They are for every woman whose pain beneath the waist is a public debate, even though it's the most intimate pain in her body. They are for the elderly woman at the grocery store who yells, "THIS IS NOT RUSSIA THIS IS NOT POLAND" when she is overcharged for a sack of potatoes. And yet she won't read this. She'll be like your parents whose excuse is always language—its lack, which is not equipped to make sense of gross abandon. She won't understand why her anger is a trophy / atrophies. Or why someone stopped feeding her chairs to sit on. Maybe you're stealing her reaction because you don't know if you're writing this for anyone. Or against.

You drip pulp over Poland's purse, contaminating the worthless currency. The sourness singes your eye, calls your attention to the floor like a slice of neon light You are inside the purse at the same time you are outside it. At the same time, you can't tell a glass of water from a glass of ocean; you have to drink to grow a mustache white with salt. At the reception, the bride and groom both take a shot of clear liquid—one water, the other vodka. Whoever swallows will be the family drunk. Swallowing is sometimes the same as traversing. Whoever swallows will be the family migrant. A tire reveals its past not by location, but wear. You have Poland's pulse tattooed on your back, and it beats behind. Your father lent his body to Communism, recited Russian in school, yet when you ask him about the woman at the grocery store, he has no idea. Time fades / both pulse and tattoo.

Your grandmother asks you to promise to not tell your grandfather the setting of your mother's rebirth. She doesn't want to be disappointed again by his absence. He is sitting, lost in thought, on a door damming the creek, a weed tickling the inside of his cheek. When she's reborn, a voice yells, "THIS IS NOT POLAND." Skeletons wearing clown masks stare down at an adult wrapped in warm sheets, like plastic left out in the sun. It will take a long time now for her to swap signatures for a sack of ocean and salt coffee to preserve it for the trip. Back to the womb. Her father lent his family her anger and stubborn determination.

A Polish family is a whirring fan, flying around, chasing each other and themselves. It isn't long before teenagers begin loitering around an abandoned cross, hanging their hats on the t, bowing to the sky spread like a picnic. They set time on fire. Not long after, the fire settles down. They have secreted duty out from their mouths, their punishment a tilt in their personalities they have to wear masks to straighten. On the train of their lives, a door is removed each time the music stops. Soon there will be a single exit, one way to die. How does one brighten up at 5am on the inside of heaven's cheek? The DNA is commonplace. A folio of love.

"Accessible abortion is essential if women are to achieve economic and political equality with men, and it is absolutely essential if the poorest, most marginalized women are to achieve economic and political equality with their middle-class sisters."

(Kitty Holland, *Repeal the 8th*)

I am afraid to read *Repeal the 8th* in Youghal, a coastal town in County Cork. The cover and binding are loud. Too soon. A barista walks by. Instinctively, I flip the book onto its belly, but there, in big bold letters, it says, "Abortion is illegal in almost every circumstance in Ireland."

What kind of activist is *this* scared?

You

"I" blares at you like a headlight, and when you close your eyes, you see a pink circle expanding, contracting, like pupils. "You" are silent.

Every essay in *Repeal the 8th* talks critically about abortion, but the critique is either preceded or followed by a personal story. Does the author think she has to write critically on her stance in order to write about her abortion? Or does she think she has to write about her abortion in order to validate her stance?

Most women featured in the book are educated. They are successful writers and journalists. They are the *control group*, no side effects, but their experiences are also real and lived in. Can good writing cancel out the need for a breadth of experiences and perspectives? Can it change people's minds in a way that poverty (pathos) can't?

These are the questions I ask, propped against a pillow that has *imagine* sewn into it in colorful lettering. Satiated by a bellyful of homemade blueberry pie.

"Most women fight wars on two fronts, one for whatever the putative topic is and one simply for the right to speak, to have ideas, to be acknowledged to be in possession of facts and truths to have value, to be a human being."

> (Rebecca Solnit, *Men Explain Things to Me*)

"Why do you think this story wasn't more queer?"

"I mean, we interviewed countless queer people, some of whom had stories that connected to consent in general. Most of those situations were with heterosexual cis men. I feel like a lot of sexual situations between queer people start as a negotiation rather than having that be an afterthought or something that comes three months down the line. Queer sex can be a lot of different things, and people each have their own definitions of what that is, so before things even happen, you're talking about what you want to have happen, what you might be into. That's not to say that violations of consent or sexual violence does not happen within queer context. Some power dynamics are a little bit more level if you're the same gender as someone else, or both are marginalized as queer individuals. Not to say that other very complex dynamics like race and class don't play into that as well."

(Kaitlin Prest, The Heart Radio – "No")

A heterosexual relationship explores opposites. Will my writing someday be categorized as pre-you and post-you?

"The life of freed instincts is composed of layers. The first layer leads to the second, the second to the

third, and so on. It leads ultimately to abnormal plea-
sures."

(Anaïs Nin, *Henry and June*)

Maybe I peeled too many layers too quickly. When
I moved west, I transplanted my ego from my body
to my soul. Porn was inevitable. A sleepless night,
endearing. When I moved even further west, another layer scraped off like bits of burnt omelet. And
then, surprisingly, I moved east. Now having lived in
four different time zones, is there any of me left? A
subscription to a threesome, bare breasts in the wil-
derness, and a book on abortion I would love Anaïs
to read.

Protesters revert? rise? strip? to their most vulnerable selves in hopes of inducing an economic stands
/ till. They wave, *No Women No Country; We Want
Doctors Not Police.* A uterus in the shape of a hanger
with an appendage that flicks off the crowd.

a) History remembers the crowd not the uterus. Or
is it the other way around? Things are always unlike what they seem. You know the saying: seeming
makes a seem out of you and me.

b) When's the last time you accurately pictured a
space before seeing it, avoiding crushing disappoint-
ment? Imagining the protests is like mentally arrang-
ing a living room. The buildings are furniture with
space to contain; outside, there's space, too, but it's
hallway space, meant to move people along. People
who picture Poland don't and then are shocked by its
beauty. But beauty, especially of cities destroyed by
war and cities preserved by war, is often a bystander
to violence. Rarely does it act, but when it does, it is
not politically correct. Process of imagination is building what is sure to suffer a process of elimination.

c) Something that can easily be torn through, like tights on sex's budget.

d) The present owns a switch on the uterus. Dark punctures the kitchen, which keeps you tired, hanging close / t eyes. You aren't a bat who's able to pray when the whole country is asleep.

e) It's not easy to drift when there's a twilight of sustenance. One does not fall asleep driving a bowl of microwavable rice. Birds do not flee a sign of bread.

f) The Polish word for "country" is *kraj*, which is pronounced "cry." Cry for *kraj*.

g) Sadly, it's only .26% of the population.

h) "Dear Polish people, keep fighting for your traditions and values. You don't have to listen to every thing [sic] this [sic] pathetic libs say." Dear Polish people, you don't have to listen to everything Mad Libs say. It's just a game for children: words finding meaning in pre-determined structures.

i) When one craves control the only thing one does with that state is suffer from it.

While the left body is dressed in black, the right body is a virginal bride, cloaked in scorching white. The country is crippled. It's the right body that has the heart, and it cradles a fetus ready to plummet, as if suddenly love were enough.

a) You like when people's clothing betrays or arouses you.

b) Sadly, love is a corridor of milk-brown doors that look friendly enough to enter but say *Employees Only*, and you, foolish you, pursued that ad on TV. As a marker of location (not the location itself), you cannot love or be loved in return.

c) This isn't to say you can't access love. More that you run mental errands or errors or detours from love, like taking hazy photos of mountains on what's supposed to be a grueling hike.

d) You need to further the female cause because *want*—if you say *want* here—would mean love controls even ambition—and is it enough?

e) You are not yet a mother, so you do not know the extent of your capacity to love. You may be talking too much about a spectrum of experience you have not had. But you know how it feels to pee on an object in hopes of procuring an odd drawing of a line. How terrifyingly political your choice to stand by your body's natural cycle: a choice of purity blackened for protest.

f) It is natural to want to scrape off the / burn white bread. It's evolutionarily about taste.

g) You no longer understand the color of Poland's population.

She's protesting because she's angry. But is her anger a self-aggrandizing dis / play of emotion or a tree that's needed to sustain life, as it traps smoke, releases oxygen. and provides cover? You lose your chance to fly your anger to meet hers, to fly over your anger. And now your anger is diluted (≠ resolved). You're left with interesting turds of phrase.

a) Jeff Probst describes the goings-on of each Survivor challenge to no one. Your couch laughs at this.

b) A survey in a women's magazine leads people to the seasonal fling that moves them closest to the sun. All this does is fool them into believing the most important questions about their bodies are being answered.

c) A complete ban would place Poland on par with two other European countries: the Vatican and Malta. Poland wouldn't yet match El Salvador, which has the harshest reproduction laws in the world: women who miscarry face forty years for aggravated murder; health professionals who carry out abortions face twelve. Upon the outbreak of the Zika virus in 2015, doctors urged women to resist pregnancy until 2018. But this proved to be no match for the biological c(l)ock

d) So resistant it's unwomanly, so unwomanly it's erratic, so erratic it's crazy, so crazy it's sarcastic, so sarcastic it's a defense mechanism, so defensive it's sexy, so sexy.

e) In the middle of a KinkBNB newsletter, it says one of their hosts was murdered by a client: "We were shocked and saddened to hear of her passing *even though it had nothing to do with our website.* Here at KinkBNB we try to give our hosts the tools to screen people coming to their dungeons, but the reality remains that for many of our hosts (who are also sex workers) violence is a fact of life."

h) Despair and ocean waves are the same emotion. They're virgins until you step in, feel the coolness of their inhale, their tickling energy. People depend on the moon to bring in romance like the tide. People depend on romance to know they are breathing. A shuttle pulls up with all the seats removed. "I'm Encyclopedia S-Z, get in."

f) The Roman Catholic Church, though fully supporting the illegality of abortion and at first upholding the 2016 ban, ultimately dismisses it for bearing too severe a punishment. For once you feel upheld by religion and become even more submissive in the past life, stringing on black thigh-high socks and kneeling slightly to the left or the right of your heart.

g) Forgiveness can be a dangerous movement into the past, and slight. A revision. And when one lingers, one starts slipping back. It is not wise to rest on a sandhill.

Would representatives ease up on reproduction / reduction laws (represent *more*) if women were open about their experiences? Roxane Gay argues women shouldn't have to give up their privacy to fight for their rights. But an only child has an abundance of privacy and then can't act. In front of an audience, she thinks about her feet and their fetal gracelessness as they shift erratically to gather height. She's *in progress* only by how she deteriorates, like a stack of half-written books in a house with moving breath.

a)   Different fruits are being carried in different trucks down different hills. The shifting has been diagnosed as a reflex to repair home / eostasis, exactly like shivering. A woman needs to shiver in order to survive This isn't a command.

b) Over one hundred attorneys sign a brief describing their abortions and deliver it to the U.S. Supreme Court. One woman is an attorney *because* of her abortion. Others recount broken cycles of poverty and teen pregnancy: *this helps your eugenics.* Months later, in the case Whole Woman's Health v. Hellerstedt. the Supreme Court rules against restrictions that place an "undue burden" on women. But what is due to women?

c) Why is maternity leave called maternity "leave" and not maternity "return"? Why is a return from maternity leave not simply "maternity return"? Why isn't abortion also "maternity leave"? Is it because motherhood cannot enter the academic species of space? It must "leave"?

d) In *The Argonauts*, Maggie Nelson talks about a lecture featuring Jane Gallop and Rosalind Krauss. Gallop showed naked photographs of herself and her son as part of a work-in-progress melding the personal to the political. Anathema! Krauss tore it apart. Nelson says, "But I was enough of a feminist to refuse any knee-jerk quarantining of the feminine or the maternal from the realm of intellectual profundity."

Many girls choose motherhood in high school. In the United States, they have the choice to mother or be finite. It isn't like they're selecting motherhood over a bouquet of flowers taped to their hips. But abortion for a teenager can be unfathomable, like needing to work a day job to support oneself as an artist; to them, you're just a talentless earthling checking toilets to make sure no blood has set in a ring.

a) The laws for parental notification for minors vary across states. Some require the minor to *notify*, some to *ask permission*. An arbitrary amount of time before the procedure: twenty-four, forty-eight hours, however much time each state deems is enough for a drive across intervention. From Minneapolis to Miami or Boston to San Francisco.

b) You look friendly, young, scared, female enough for intervention—a terminal invention.

c) You, for example, wouldn't have chosen abortion when you were sixteen, yet now it seems plausible, like choosing to speak another language in a roomful of people, knowing you would both benefit from and be punished for passing by their cluttered well of understanding.

d) If she chooses to be a mother, give up coffee with her when she's pregnant. And alcohol and cigarettes and Adderall and pot. And cleaning the cat litter and dying your hair. Purchase a well-fitting bra, OK? Or else she'll grow to resent you, and her child will grow too.

No more periods—what if that were the meaning of celibacy? What if women could choose to bleed if fertility was their thing or p / urge if it wasn't? They could choose to no longer understand the brand *Always*. Always choose to no longer understand. Are condoms or tampons more expensive? More responsible. You can only buy one. One of you. They're both going up one of you: the blood and the urge. Your friends are calling from karaoke, and you also have a mouth to fill. You're bleeding, but it isn't urgent.

a) ~ 10% of American girls begin to menstruate before the age of eight. Imagine asking a child if bleeding is her thing: hey Amalya, hey Amethyst, hey America, do you appreciate faucets when they drip coolly like pesticides and maybe also the handyman when he crawls around in your pipes, digging his nails into your frontal feces? He wants you to believe he's fixing them until one day he sets up a cubicle there, paints it brown, and hangs framed pictures of him and his wife. "Brown is a sturdy color," you say, slowly accepting the tattered second-hand couch.

b) The night he breaks your heart for a second time you can't sleep, so you break bread with windows and watch rain-blurred light walk people home. How it sets winter on fire.

c) "Many prostitutes don't take time off for their period. They either wedge cotton balls up against their cervix or take birth control pills to control menstruation." Another website confesses to red condoms and dimmed lights to disguise the blood.

d) A dip in snow doesn't wash blood white. A dip in snow smells of dirt and dog piss and a little girl's tongue. A dip in stains knows it through the nose.

At a hip coffee shop, the floor is white hexagonal tiles, which are periodically and randomly replaced by black. This could be *1 out of 50 women*. Like the Holocaust Memorial in Berlin, which is a field of gray stone blocks that could be vertical graves or a bar graph indicating how many dead or any number of things. It turns out architects have the biggest secrets. They are taken to disaster, like an emergency vehicle with its sails lifted by a heavy wind. At the Memorial, little girls with black ponytails scam your friend out of five euros and you, your favorite pen. They wouldn't give it back, even after you asked. It makes you wonder what, if anything, they get for bringing back a pen: more valuable than a rubber band but less than a watch. It's an American pen. People have died by American pens.

a) As you powerwalk down the backstreet abortions, you crowd your possessions closer to your chest. Your eyes dart around the women's faces, hoping to avoid locking eyes. The ones who have been ripped open are lined up like sandbags, the flood being too expensive to fight with anything but their bodies. The others are singing-praying-begging for the opposite of money, a tool for elimination. Begging for money, a tool for elimination.

b) There are "less" safe methods, meaning unprofessionally administered or outdated, and "least" safe methods, meaning nothing.

c) You dream your mother is horrified a droplet of

water will touch her bellybutton. She doesn't want anything to harm the baby. But the ocean has already skinned you on your deep way in, drowning your ticking heart.

d) Ectopic. from *ectopia*, "morbid displacement of parts," from *ektopos*, "away from a place, distant; foreign, strange," from *ek-*, "out" and *topos*, "place." An immigrant is ectopic. Growing where it shouldn't.

e) Dust appears gray because it's mostly dead skin. You're graying when you die and dying when you gray. Your body's in a state of *interpreting*.

f) Who even has choices? Not the female patient, not the female doctor, not even the male doctor, but maybe the male patient. Maybe the mail carrier but even he cannot choose what he carries. You wait at the foot of the bed for an uncomplicated delivery but soon hear from a neighbor that the mail carrier was shot; the packages might or might not have survived. In yoga, if you can't see your toes, your body's misaligned. Maladapted to freedom like a woman.

g) A teaspoon of sugar lands in the doctor's *filiżanka*; she's seduced by the Polish word for "mug." Frère Jacques. She's a full baptized Catholic—drink her up—but she has her doubts. She begins to wonder about the Polish language, if it can properly communicate loss. Why is *kawa* (coffee) half of *kawałek* (piece). If coffee is half of a piece of peace, what is the other.

h) Slip her something extra to perform the abortion. She knows slipping money through a vacuum to the womb will save her (their) body from slipping into a coma.

i) "The architects say to the doctors, at least you can bury your mistakes" (Donna Stonecipher, *Transaction Histories*).

j) A doctor interviewed by BBC News says, "If I have a patient with pre-eclampsia, who is 32 weeks pregnant, I will have to let her and her child die." Pre-eclampsia means a placenta isn't functioning properly, and it's marked by high blood-pressure and protein in the urine. The only cure is timely delivery of the baby and the sac. But, in cases where abortion is illegal, if the baby isn't mature enough to survive post-delivery, the mother will be forced to keep it, killing her own chances of survival.

k) She is afraid to survive following delivery. Friendly but scared and exhausted, she pulls up to an orange diamond flapping in the wind: *Men Working*. A witching insomnia rips through the city, unzipping its good mood.

l) A friend says, "These poems are good and all, but they won't save lives." Despite this, you think poetry tells you to live. Medicine only does it.

During a miscarriage, the fetus burns through layers like a Matryoshka doll: first the mother then the earth. Its mother burns too, she burns, she burns; she is thrown from the fire like from a socket. Men she does business with ask if they can first meet her husband. They fear she'll run on, so they give her a period. Her mis / demeanor has changed. She is no longer Mr. Nice Guy, high-fiving the / ir assholes. A baby / carriage sits unattended while she takes her first sip of leather in months. She is now an alcoholic. An illegal guardian. Biodegradable. It's one thing to scrape, another to scrap her interior.

a) A man comes home interrupting her pregnancy. He's a detective. Not her husband, just her detective. Knowing that especially unexpected blood smells metallic, he puts her under arrest, meaning she doesn't get to. Rest. A virile virulent womb doesn't deserve it.

b) In a Starbucks bathroom in Budapest, you open yourself to find what looks like a chewed-up glob of red Skittles the size of a thumb. You poke at it like a child pokes at bugs to see if they'll move, then frantically google what everything in the world looks like, hoping to find a picture that matches. Nothing does. Back in your apartment, you try again, but it's hard to match pictures of blood clots and fetuses. They're unique, like eyes.

c) Pregnancy carries the body on the wing of a pinecone, poking through translucent snow. Pregnancy is a tripping hazard. Everyone notices it and waves because secretly everyone wants to be seated on the royal pinecone.

d) The number of kids one has is equal to how many parts, how many lines in this world's play.

e) A frat man flings his melted Dairy Queen out the window of his car, and it explodes on your shoulder. You can complain when what happens is a coincidence. Your pain doubles.

f) She talks about her miscarriage on the phone with a friend who says, "Your offering is mesmerizing." The friend compares pregnancy to a hand-written letter. Sometimes the seal breaks. Sometimes the gods steal it, or other women find it—not necessarily the wrong women. And "sometimes mothers are selfish and wrap three lines of duct tape around their litter, but you, my friend, you offer yours up."

g) In Polish, the word for "miscarriage" is also the word for "abortion." *Poronienie*, where *nie* is the word for "no."

h) Mid-birth follows the progressive dilation of the cervix and precedes the delivery of the placenta. It follows opening and precedes the final release.

i) No one can predict surviving a child. Except when one can. Predict surviving a dream.

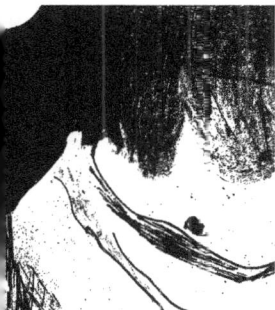

The solution comes to you in a dream. If choosing
from the nouns, it would be "banana-yellow eggs."
The dream touches down weeks after the dream: it
is up to you to spoil Game of Thrones. A fetus whose
mother chooses to abort but cannot spoils (her).

spoil: Craster / to damage severely or harm

spoil: Drogo / archaic. to take or seize by force

*spoil: Joffrey Baratheon / archaic. to strip of good(s),
value(ables)*

spoil: Stanis Baratheon / an act of plundering

spoil: Tywin Lannister / an object of (p)lun(derin)g

spoil: Shae / booty taken in war or robbery

spoil: Ygritte / an imperfectly made object, damaged

spoil: Talisa Stark / to plunder, pillage, or rob

spoil: Robb Stark / be spoiling for, informal. to be very eager for; be desirous of:

spoil: Jaime / waste material, as that which is cast up in excavating

spoil: The Hound / to diminish or impair the quality of

spoil: Euron / to impair the character or nature of someone by unwise treatment, excessive indulgence, etc.

spoil: Daenerys / to become bad, or unfit for use, as perishable substances; become tainted or putrid

On February 1, 2017, an ice storm settles on my glasses. As my fingertips blink to break themselves open, an elementary school comes into view, one I've passed dozens of times on my way to the coffee shop where art in every language hangs on the walls. A storm of mountains makes up my left peripheral view, though if I were smarter and turned back, it would make up my right. Hence, a little girl does not make it home. She survives everything she has learned. She continues to survive where she has learned how to make history. *Remembers the harshest reproduction laws in your country. How did you contribute?* The school I pass serves as a social instrument. Little girls interact with little boys and girls every day. The learning that goes on sources its material internally.

I'll be leaving school for the first time since I entered the first grade without a word of English to my name, and I am afraid. I cannot plan for how I'll maintain the socially fueled political structures that exist in school without constantly behaving historically (eventfully). How can I see my community every day as an adult, have the conversations and participate in the events that connect me to those fighting in whatever way is available to them in the moment, for issues that surpass their tolerance for apathy . . .

. . . breaking open, I pass a man who is pointing binoculars into a tree, which is actually a woman's bedroom. He looks over in my direction and immediately defends himself: "I'm watchin' for squirrels." I find this humorous enough but feel gratitude bubbling up inside. Presumably because I am a woman, he assumes I am on her side, whoever she is. *Remember the harshest reproduction laws in your country.* Maybe this is progress: a male-bodied individual believing two female-bodied individuals are capable of behaving as allies. *In your eyes.*

It's easier to say the war has ended. It's easier to say, "I'm not afraid my kid's a woman's body." What's there to do with bodies that are pieces other than try to put them together or pretend they are already whole?

But history remembers the harshest reproduction. It's why the Vatican invests so much interest in a woman's tears. Female bodies are broken by laws and then set free to pacify the feeling, thinking beings inside them. Sometimes they split into fragments that are their children. Intertwining legs with their grandmothers, they prepare for a cold war. When this proves fundamental, they're right with their history. *Remembers the harshest reproduction laws in your country. In their* eyes. And the government doesn't want that.

War breaks out as an intersection flung on the female form. People cross there. Little female forms in training wheels turn their already educated heads. Maybe there's a stoplight. Maybe it turns green when she decides something for herself, red when progress pays underhand. An accident is bound to happen. A vehicle speeds through red and gets away with it. Anyway. It's for your own good. Anyway. It's for your protection. Otherwise, you'd move traffic through tar. Anyway. Maybe a stoplight doesn't exist, and everything mobilizes as a boundless mess. Everyone's mind narrows when it approaches something extra to have to learn to understand. Moving across a woman's body shouldn't mean uncovering plot on which to settle. It should mean mapping the bone that's already there and speaking with the realtor about who can move in.

A couple nights following the 2016 election, I dream a friend and I are kidnapped, taken to a worn-down house that, despite its history (*remembers the harshest reproduction laws in your country*) glows like a band-aid in the sun. An older man strips us in familiar, yet peculiar ways and then slowly preps his cock for the rape. I am terrified and harmless. Then, another man resembling the rapist who we figure is the man's son bursts in and attacks him. The men fight, juggling their limbs, but ultimately, the rapist escapes his son's grasp and races to his beat-up car. We hear it reluctantly chug downhill away from the house. The rapist's son unties us and leads us outside, where he hands me a purple dildo. I throw it in the direction of the chunky car, and as it maneuvers down the road, it grows bigger and bigger until it grows big enough to off-road the vehicle and eject its passenger.

For days following the dream, I see everything as needing a large, purple dildo: a male student unable to find his voice in conversations about sexism, the insanely huggable comfort of Fruit of the Loom boxers, a text here and there from my soon-to-be-ex partner, the simile: *as unfair as an orgasm during rape.* The rapist represents the present political climate: an unwelcome penetration into the history (*remembers the harshest reproduction laws*) of my body, as if it were taking photographs of me, my mother, and my grandmother for personal use. The dream suggests I should fight fire with fire, or rather, rape with a large, purple dildo.

Then I join a group a women who are talking about their vaginas or their reasons for showing up to talk about their vaginas. I don't say anything, embarrassed of large, purple dildidis, but I understand that my thinking on the dream has been backwards. I am not supposed to fight fire with fire. This detachable, flexible purple leg that exists purely for female pleasure is the representation of something rather than the thing itself; the right people could right (write) representation. I am supposed to fight fire with water.

Now, in the summer of 2019, at the dawn of a new presidential election, I watch every Democratic debate, afraid to lose out on knowledge and opportunity. I nurture a close network of friends who live in different cities across the world. We manufacture purple dildos through our collective activism. Having this book underfoot feels like a cold stream of water, soothing my mind, body, and soul. And ultimately my guilt. This is how I fight.

The day of the ice storm, I step on a bus and travel to a place where it's sixty degrees, and winter branches break open to lay bare thousands of seashells, their surfaces slick with fluids and tied to little bones. A body stalks the gardens, her left hand clasping a rail for balance and her right, periodically reaching between her legs (home) as she searches for the seashell that feels most like her vagina. She does this because she wants an artifact to cherish, her original vagina swimming in history. *Remembers the harshest reproduction laws in its eyes.* The eye of the seashell bleeds when matched correctly, representing either her injured foot or their period, the people's. It doesn't go to war as a punctuation mark indicating weakness, but as a flood signifying strength.

On January 21st, 2017, some 3.3 million Americans act in an event they call "The Women's March." The March on Washington counts more than three times the participants than those at the president's inauguration the day before. Over five hundred marches occur in the U.S. alone, and across all seven continents. Their cause: history remembers the harshest reproduction laws in my country. In my eyes.

Everyone waves signs: *a woman without a man is like a fish without a bicycle, the only minority ruining America is the rich, we need to talk about the elephant in the womb,* and *yea I chase pussy, but I also fight for her rights.* For once, I'm there as primary source material, and I'm angry. We're all mad here, mandated to learn in *his* classroom, though history (*remembers*) is a social institution. We'll go on pitching large, purple dildos into the world and doing everything but simply waiting to see if they will off-road the war.

We concretize a plan to love what's absent

red.

"I could not stop her from giving birth to herself if I tried" is from Bhanu Kapil's *Incubation: a Space for Monsters*

"This is neither a time nor a place" is borrowed from Ben Lerner's *Angle of Yaw*

"I have agreed not to defend Poland from the east / I have agreed not to defend Poland from the East" is from Ben Lerner's *Angle of Yaw*

Others:

"Abortion issue threatens Polish admission to EU." *The Guardian.*
"Apelują o dopisanie klauzuli sumienia do ustawy o zawodzie farmaceuty." mgr.farm.
Camus, Albert. *The Myth of Sisyphus.*
"Catholic head of hospital fired over refusal to abort a deformed fetus." The Globe and Mail.
Caytas, Joanna Diane. "Women's Reproductive Rights as a Political Price of Post-communist Trans-

formation in Poland." *Amsterdam Law Forum.*

Chapman, Annabelle. "Poland's Law and Justice party has triumphed again by fusing left and right." *New Statesman America.*

"Childbirth Stage 2: Pushing the Baby Out." whattoexpect.com.

Cummings McLean, Dorothy. "Polish government stalling on 'Stop abortion' bill." *LifeSiteNews.*

"The doctors' declaration of faith." *The Economist.*

Engelberg, Stephen. "Poland Acts to Curb Abortion; Church Seeks Ban." *The New York Times.*

Fuszara, Małgorzata. "Legal Regulation of Abortion in Poland." *University of Chicago Press Journals.*

Gorman, Andree. "The 9 countries with the most draconian abortion laws in the world." *Business Insider.*

Haltiwanger, John. "4 Amazing Statistics About The Women's March." *Elite Daily.*

Henley, Jon. "Election results give hope to opposition in Poland and Hungary." *The Guardian.*

Henley, Jon and Christian Davies. "Poland's populist Law and Justice party win second term in power." *The Guardian.*

Hirvonen, Ewa. *Polish Abortion Tourism.*

Jacobsen, JL. "Out from behind the contraceptive Iron Curtain." *World Watch*, National Center for Biotechnology Information.

Lopez, Shane J. "Where Does Your Hope Come From?" *Psychology Today.*

Noack, Rick. "Polish women go on nationwide strike against proposed abortion ban." *The Washington Post.*

Nowicka, Wanda. "The Struggle for Abortion Rights in Poland." sxpolitics.org.

"Number of passenger cars per 1,000 inhabitants in Poland between 1990 and 2017." statista.com.

"Parental Consent and Notification Laws." Planned Parenthood.

"Poland abortion: Parliament rejects near-total ban." *BBC News.*

"Poland's abortion ban proposal near collapse after mass protests." *The Guardian.*

Półtauska, Wanda. "Declaration of faith of Catholic doctors and students of medicine, on the sexuality and fertility of human beings." *The Linacre Quarterly*, National Center for Biotechnology Information.

Ramet, Sabrina P. *The Catholic Church in Polish History: From 966 to the Present.*

Roache, Madeline. "Poland Is Trying to Make Abortion Dangerous, Illegal, and Impossible." *Foreign Policy.*

Santora, Marc and Joanna Berendt. "Polish Women Protest Proposed Abortion Ban (Again)." *The New York Times.*

Scutti, Susan. "Puberty comes earlier and earlier for girls." *Newsweek.*

Shubert, Atika and Antonia Mortensen. "As Poland mulls new abortion bill, women head to Germany." *CNN.*

"Stop bezprawnemu ograniczaniu dostępu do
    antykoncepcji!" naszademokracja.pl.
Tietze, Christopher. "Abortion in Europe." *AJPH: a
    publication of the American Public Health
    Association.*
"Zobacz, co pisał 'Gość Niedzielny' o Alicji Tysiąc."
    Gazeta.pl.

And:

a copy of the 1993 "anti-abortion" act was found on reproductiverights.org

the fact sheet for the case Tysiąc v Poland was found on reproductiverights.org

a copy of the "declaration of faith" was found on polskatimes.pl

federa.org.pl (Federacja na rzecz Kobiet i Planowania Rodziny), #HISTORIEKOBIET

a copy of the 2016 "stop abortion" bill was found on stronazycia pl

a copy of the statement "Polish Parliament Must Protect Women's Health and Rights" was found on reproductiverights.org

thebarrenyears.wordpress.com

a copy of the brief Whole Woman's Health v Heller-

Thank you to the editors of the journals where certain sections of this book appeared previously, sometimes in slightly altered forms:

Adirondack Review: "You listen to an interview with a woman deported to Mexico..." as "Container Laws"

A Velvet Giant: "Czerń"

Bookends Review: "No More Expologies"

Thank you also to the artist residencies where I composed the majority of this book:

Brashnar Creative Project in Skopje, Macedonia

Bridge Guard in Štúrovo, Slovakia

Greywood Arts in Killeagh, Ireland

I am incredibly thankful to everyone who helped make this book a reality. Thank you to J'Lyn Chapman who convinced me the manuscript I brought to her was actually two books, which became *Polalka* and *Notes for Mid-Birth*. Thank you to Ryan Mihaly for reading many drafts of this book and ridding it of redundancies unseen by the person looking. And a special thank you to Inside the Castle who believed in this book when it was still bare-boned and disorganized and worked with me every step of the way to its completion. Thank you also to the friends who heard my anger, my guilt, and my attempts at personal (and political) resolution. You are my strength and joy.

www.ingramcontent.com/pod-product-compliance
Lightning Source LLC
Chambersburg PA
CBHW020251030426
42336CB00010B/719